CHALLENGES OF RECRUITING AND RETAINING A CYBERSECURITY WORK FORCE

HEARING

BEFORE THE

SUBCOMMITTEE ON CYBERSECURITY AND INFRASTRUCTURE PROTECTION

OF THE

COMMITTEE ON HOMELAND SECURITY
HOUSE OF REPRESENTATIVES

ONE HUNDRED FIFTEENTH CONGRESS

FIRST SESSION

SEPTEMBER 7, 2017

Serial No. 115–26

Printed for the use of the Committee on Homeland Security

Available via the World Wide Web: http://www.govinfo.gov

U.S. GOVERNMENT PUBLISHING OFFICE

28–415 PDF   WASHINGTON : 2018

COMMITTEE ON HOMELAND SECURITY

MICHAEL T. MCCAUL, Texas, *Chairman*

LAMAR SMITH, Texas
PETER T. KING, New York
MIKE ROGERS, Alabama
JEFF DUNCAN, South Carolina
LOU BARLETTA, Pennsylvania
SCOTT PERRY, Pennsylvania
JOHN KATKO, New York
WILL HURD, Texas
MARTHA MCSALLY, Arizona
JOHN RATCLIFFE, Texas
DANIEL M. DONOVAN, JR., New York
MIKE GALLAGHER, Wisconsin
CLAY HIGGINS, Louisiana
JOHN H. RUTHERFORD, Florida
THOMAS A. GARRETT, JR., Virginia
BRIAN K. FITZPATRICK, Pennsylvania
RON ESTES, Kansas

BENNIE G. THOMPSON, Mississippi
SHEILA JACKSON LEE, Texas
JAMES R. LANGEVIN, Rhode Island
CEDRIC L. RICHMOND, Louisiana
WILLIAM R. KEATING, Massachusetts
DONALD M. PAYNE, JR., New Jersey
FILEMON VELA, Texas
BONNIE WATSON COLEMAN, New Jersey
KATHLEEN M. RICE, New York
J. LUIS CORREA, California
VAL BUTLER DEMINGS, Florida
NANETTE DIAZ BARRAGÁN, California

BRENDAN P. SHIELDS, *Staff Director*
STEVEN S. GIAIER, *Deputy Chief Counsel*
MICHAEL S. TWINCHEK, *Chief Clerk*
HOPE GOINS, *Minority Staff Director*

SUBCOMMITTEE ON CYBERSECURITY AND INFRASTRUCTURE PROTECTION

JOHN RATCLIFFE, Texas, *Chairman*

JOHN KATKO, New York
DANIEL M. DONOVAN, JR., New York
MIKE GALLAGHER, Wisconsin
THOMAS A. GARRETT, JR., Virginia
BRIAN K. FITZPATRICK, Pennsylvania
MICHAEL T. MCCAUL, Texas *(ex officio)*

CEDRIC L. RICHMOND, Louisiana
SHEILA JACKSON LEE, Texas
JAMES R. LANGEVIN, Rhode Island
VAL BUTLER DEMINGS, Florida
BENNIE G. THOMPSON, Mississippi *(ex officio)*

KRISTEN M. DUNCAN, *Subcommittee Staff Director*

CONTENTS

Page

CHALLENGES OF RECRUITING AND RETAINING A CYBERSECURITY WORK FORCE

Thursday, September 7, 2017

U.S. House of Representatives,
Committee on Homeland Security,
Subcommittee on Cybersecurity and
Infrastructure Protection,
Washington, DC.

The subcommittee met, pursuant to notice, at 3:14 p.m., in room HVC–210, Capitol Visitor Center, Hon. John Ratcliffe (Chairman of the subcommittee) presiding.

Present: Representatives Ratcliffe, Fitzpatrick, Katko, Richmond, Demings, and Langevin.

Also present: Representative Barragán.

Mr. RATCLIFFE. The Committee on Homeland Security Subcommittee on Cybersecurity and Infrastructure Protection will come to order.

The subcommittee is meeting today to receive testimony regarding the challenges of recruiting and retaining a cybersecurity work force.

I now recognize myself for an opening statement.

Good afternoon. I would like to begin by thanking our panel for taking the time today to be here to testify. I appreciate your patience as we just finished up a vote series. I am glad that you waited for us. Your thoughts and your opinions are very important to us and will help inform us as we oversee the Department of Homeland Security in meeting its cybersecurity work force challenges.

Cybersecurity is one of the most daunting National security and economic security challenges of our generation. As our adversaries grow in sophistication, so, too, will the challenges associated with preventing their attacks.

My colleagues on this committee have heard me say this often, but I will say it again. America will remain the world superpower only so long as it remains the world cybersecurity superpower.

As the lead civilian agency for our Federal cybersecurity posture, the Department of Homeland Security factors as a critical piece of this equation. It is a tremendous privilege to chair this subcommittee and I look forward to our continued partnership with the private sector and the administration on these important cybersecurity issues, because inaction is simply not an option.

In 2014, it was estimated that $1 billion of personally identifiable information was stolen from cyber attacks. It is also estimated that the average cost of a data breach will be $150 million by 2020. Cyber attacks are growing in frequency and they are growing in their sophistication, but the availability of qualified cybersecurity professionals to deal with these challenges is unfortunately not keeping pace.

There have been several studies over the past few years documenting the growing shortage of cybersecurity professionals. In this ever-increasingly connected world, the problem is only going to get worse. One estimate from the consulting firm of Frost & Sullivan is forecasting a shortage of a staggering 1.8 million cybersecurity workers world-wide by 2022, just 5 years from now.

Some industry estimates are that 53 percent of organizations now experience delays of 6 months or longer to find qualified cybersecurity candidates. We know that the entire industry is facing an unprecedented shortage of cybersecurity workers at all levels of competency, from front-line defenders to CIOs.

It is against this backdrop that the Department of Homeland Security must compete with the private sector to recruit and retain the best talent possible in order to carry out its cybersecurity mission and to protect our critical infrastructure. Unfortunately, DHS's issues are compounded by the additional hiring challenges often felt by the Federal Government.

DHS must work to overcome slow hiring processes and work force supply and pipeline issues in order to build the essential work force required to meet its cyber mission. DHS must strategically plan for the training, recruitment, and the retention of its cybersecurity work force.

The Homeland Security Committee passed several pieces of legislation that were signed into law to augment the cybersecurity work force at DHS, including the Border Patrol Agent Pay Reform Act of 2014 that expanded DHS's hiring authorities allowing the Department to better recruit and hire qualified cyber professionals. Unfortunately, these new authorities have not yet been fully implemented.

This is an area where hearing from the experts before us today will provide valuable input as we conduct oversight of DHS's responsibilities and ensure that DHS has the human capital and resources necessary to carry out its important cybersecurity mission.

The Federal Government supports a number of programs to recruit and retain its work force. In particular, the CyberCorps Scholarship for Service Program was authorized in the National Cybersecurity Enhancement Act of 2014 and focuses on recruiting and training the next generation of information technology professionals, industry control system security professionals, and security managers.

Working with DHS, the National Science Foundation has awarded grants for the CyberCorps Scholarship for Service Program since 2011 to increase and strengthen Federal, State, local, Tribal, and territorial governments' cyber work force. As of January 2017, there were 69 active Scholarship for Service institutions, including eight in my home State of Texas. CyberCorps has provided scholarships to 2,945 recipients with 2,223 graduates serving Federal, State, local, Tribal, and territorial governments and 623 students are currently working toward that goal.

The recent interest my office has received from both 2- and 4-year colleges in my district about participating in the CyberCorps program is encouraging. It reinforces that stakeholders of all sizes, from all corners of the country want to be part of the cybersecurity work force solution.

I look forward to a robust conversation with our distinguished panel of witnesses today that will support our efforts in strengthening DHS's effort to recruit and retain talented cybersecurity professionals.

The Chair now recognizes the Ranking Minority Member of the subcommittee, the gentleman from Louisiana, Mr. Richmond.

[The statement of Mr. Ratcliffe follows:]

STATEMENT OF CHAIRMAN JOHN RATCLIFFE

SEPTEMBER 7, 2017

Good afternoon.

I would like to begin by thanking our panel for taking the time today to testify. Your thoughts and opinions are very important as we oversee the Department of Homeland Security in meeting its cybersecurity work force challenges.

Cybersecurity is one of the most daunting challenges of our generation, and as our adversaries grow in sophistication, so will the challenges associated with preventing their attacks. My colleagues on this committee have heard me say this often, but I'll say it again—America will only remain the world's superpower so long as it remains the world's cybersecurity superpower.

As the lead civilian agency for our Federal cybersecurity posture, DHS factors as a critical piece of this equation. It is a great privilege to chair this subcommittee, and I look forward to our continued partnership with the private sector and the administration on these important cybersecurity issues.

Because inaction is simply not an option.

According to the Cisco 2017 Annual Cybersecurity Report, ransomware is growing at a yearly rate of 350 percent and the firm Cybersecurity Ventures predicts cyber crime will cost the world in excess of $6 trillion annually by 2021, making it more profitable than the global trade of all major illegal drugs combined. It is also estimated that the average cost of a data breach will be $150 million by 2020. Cyber attacks are growing in frequency and sophistication, but the availability of qualified cybersecurity professionals to deal with these challenges is not keeping pace.

There have been several studies over the past few years documenting the growing shortage of cybersecurity professionals. In this ever-increasing connected world, the problem is only going to get worse. Today, one estimate, from the consulting firm Frost & Sullivan, is forecasting a shortage of a staggering 1.8 million cybersecurity workers world-wide by 2022. One industry organization estimates that 53 percent of organizations experience delays of 6 months or longer to find qualified cybersecurity candidates.

We know that the entire industry is facing an unprecedented shortage of cybersecurity workers at all levels of competency—from front-line defenders to CIOs. Against this backdrop, the Department of Homeland Security must compete with the private sector to recruit and retain the best talent possible in order to carry out its cybersecurity mission and protect our critical infrastructure.

Unfortunately, DHS's issues are compounded by additional hiring challenges often felt by the Federal Government. DHS must work to overcome slow hiring processes and work force supply and pipeline issues in order to build the essential work force required to meet its cyber mission. DHS must strategically plan for the training, recruitment, and retention of its cybersecurity work force.

The Homeland Security Committee passed several pieces of legislation that were signed into law to augment the cybersecurity work force at DHS, including the Border Patrol Agent Pay Reform Act of 2014 that expanded DHS's hiring authorities, allowing the Department to better recruit and hire qualified cyber professionals. Unfortunately, these new authorities have not yet been fully implemented. This is an area where hearing from the experts before us today will provide valuable input as we conduct oversight of DHS's responsibilities and ensure that DHS has the human capital and resources necessary to carry out its important cybersecurity mission.

The Federal Government supports a number of programs to recruit and retain its work force. In particular, the CyberCorps: Scholarship-For-Service Program was authorized in the National Cybersecurity Enhancement Act of 2014 and focuses on recruiting and training the next generation of information technology professionals, industrial control system security professionals, and security managers.

Working with DHS, the National Science Foundation has awarded grants for the CyberCorps: Scholarship-For-Service program since 2011 to increase and strengthen Federal, State, local, Tribal, and territorial governments' cyber work force. As of January 2017, there were 69 active Scholarship for Service institutions, including 8 in my home State of Texas. CyberCorps has provided scholarships to 2,945 recipients, with 2,223 graduates serving Federal, State, local, Tribal, and territorial governments and 623 students currently working toward that goal.

The recent interest my office has received from 2- and 4-year colleges in my district about participating in the CyberCorps program is encouraging. It reinforces that stakeholders of all sizes from all corners of the country want to be part of the cybersecurity work force solution.

I look forward to a robust conversation with our distinguished panel of witnesses that will support our efforts in strengthening DHS's efforts to recruit and retain talented cybersecurity professionals.

Mr. RICHMOND. Let me first thank the Chairman for holding this hearing because our Nation faces an evolving array of cyber threats and it is crucial that we have a robust, talented cybersecurity work force.

For some time now, experts have predicted that the demand for cybersecurity professionals was quickly outpacing our supply. In 2012, the Bureau of Labor Statistics projected that by 2020 there would be 400,000 computer scientists available to fill 1.4 million computer science jobs. Recent estimates suggest that the deficit is growing instead of shrinking and may reach 1.8 million by 2022.

Let's be clear: This is nothing short of a threat to our National security.

These are the professionals we rely on to help us prepare for and respond to the next WannaCry, Mirai, or Fancy Bear. These are the people who will prevent State-sponsored hackers from taking down our electrical grid or infiltrating our State election systems. These are the experts we need to stand on the front lines during a major cyber attack and make sure we have functioning hospitals, banks, transportation systems, and lines of communication.

We need cybersecurity professionals in the private sector protecting our intellectual property and personal data, and we need them in the public sector protecting our Nation's most sensitive intelligence. Yet we know that the Federal Government and DHS in particular is struggling to compete with the private sector for cyber talent.

What is more, this administration has failed to fill even the most critical, senior-level, cybersecurity posts, asking agencies like DHS's National Programs and Protections Directorate to carry out broad, complex cybersecurity missions without a permanent under secretary. This lack of leadership makes us vulnerable.

We should be doing everything we can to right-size our cybersecurity labor force. There is a lot more we can do. We need to introduce students to computers before they get to college, even the ones who go to schools that can't afford expensive tech programs and specialized instructors. I also believe there is untapped potential in vocational schools, 2-year programs, minority-serving institutions, and our historically black colleges and universities.

Once we have figured out how to get more people to choose cybersecurity as a career, we need to convince them to turn down a higher-paying job and spend some time in Federal service.

Within the Federal Government, we need to promote recruitment and retention programs, particularly at DHS which has lagged behind other cyber-focused Federal agencies like the NSA or FBI in attracting cyber talent. For its part, DHS needs to be more forward-thinking and learn to anticipate the needs of an evolving work force that values professional development, a flexible work culture, the ability to transition in and out of positions or even fields.

In closing, there is no question that the cyber work force challenge is a daunting one, but the stakes are too high for us to ignore it. Last year, the global economy lost over $450 billion to cyber criminals and over 2 billion personal records were stolen in the United States alone. Meanwhile, studies show that less than half of United States' businesses would say that they are prepared for a cyber attack, and that small Main Street businesses are struggling the most.

I look forward to hearing the testimony of our witnesses today and hope we can identify innovative ways to work together to address cybersecurity work force challenges.

Mr. Chairman, before I yield back, I would like to submit for the record from Wesley Simpson, chief operating officer of (ISC)², along with the 2017 Global Information Security Workforce Study: Women in Cybersecurity; and the report the 2017 Global Information Security Workforce Study: U.S. Federal Government Results.

Mr. RATCLIFFE. Without objection.

[The information referred to follows:]

STATEMENT OF WESLEY SIMPSON, CISSP AND CHIEF OPERATING OFFICER, (ISC)²

SEPTEMBER 7, 2017

Chairman Ratcliffe, Ranking Member Richmond, Members of the subcommittee, thank you for the opportunity to provide written testimony for today's hearing titled Challenges of Recruiting and Retaining a Cyber Workforce. This hearing is an important one as it highlights a critical work force and ultimately a critical National security challenge that we face: Ensuring that we are training enough cybersecurity professionals to address the current and projected work force shortage in the public and private sector.

My name is Wesley Simpson and I am the chief operating officer of the International Information System Security Certification Consortium, commonly known as (ISC)², the world's leading cybersecurity and IT security professional organization. We are an international, non-profit membership association for information security leaders. We have 125,000 members world-wide and continue to grow just as the cyber work force needs grow.

In addition to the training and certification work that we do, including the internationally recognized CISSP certification, we are also committed to education of the general public through our support for the Center for Cyber Safety and Education. We believe it is crucial not only to close the current gap in cybersecurity professionals, but we must also do so in a diverse way bringing more women and minorities into the field of cybersecurity. Information on our work with the Center for Cyber Safety and Education can be found at *www.iamcybersafe.org*.

Earlier this year, (ISC)² in partnership with the Center for Cyber Safety and Education, Booz Allen, Frost & Sullivan and Alta Associates released the 2017 Global Information Security Workforce Study. This is the 8th biennial release of the study and the largest to date. We surveyed 19,641 cyber professionals representing 170 countries. This included 2,620 professionals from the U.S. Federal Government.

According to our survey we are on pace to reach a cyber work force gap of 1.8 million jobs by 2022—a stunning 20% increase from our forecast made in 2015. As part of our study, we also segmented out the data for certain demographic groups and I will provide information around the Government work force, and women in the cyber work force later in my remarks.

Globally, our survey found that 66% of information security workers said their staffs are short-handed—too few professionals to address the threats they encountered. That's an increase of 4 percent from the 2015 survey. This number jumps to 68% when you consider only respondents from North America.

Workers cite a number of reasons for the current shortage. These include: Qualified personnel are difficult to find; work force requirements are not understood by leadership; business conditions can't support hiring additional personnel; security workers are difficult to retain; and a belief that there is no clear information security career path.

On the positive side, 70% of hiring managers surveyed are looking to increase their work force. In fact, 30% are planning to increase that work force by 20% or more. This is most evident in the fields of health care, retail, and manufacturing. So the job opportunities are there. In addition, fully 87% of cyber professionals started out in a different career. While most came from IT, a number come from other career fields. For North America, about 35% started in a different field. This indicates that training, retraining programs, and certification programs are working and are necessary to help close the current work force gap.

Let me now turn to some of the segments that we examined within the larger data set, starting with the Federal Government. Overall there is some good news in the Government data. Half of the respondents feel that Government security has improved. This is due to improved security awareness, improved understanding of risk management and effective security standards. Some 36% believe that it the level of Government security has stayed the same, and 4% believe that Government security has gotten worse. Of those that felt the situation has gotten worse, they cited the need for more qualified professionals, adequate funding, and better security standards. In addition, respondents felt that the most important factor in securing an organization's infrastructure is the hiring and retaining of qualified information security professionals.

We also asked about the key factors in retaining Government information security professionals. Interestingly, the top two responses were not directly related to compensation, but rather focused on training and certification. Respondents wanted the Government to offer training programs and to pay for cyber certifications. This was followed by improving compensation packages, flexible work schedules, and supporting remote/flexible working. So you can see that while compensation is important, other factors rise to the top in terms of retaining talent in the Government work force. When looking at incentives for new hires, we see a similar trend, with certification, training, and education reimbursement as the most effective recruitment tool followed by flexible work schedule.

Let me close on this segment by providing three additional findings that are relevant to the question of attracting and retaining cyber professionals. First, 78% of respondents felt that greatest demand for new hires is in nonmanagerial staff. Second, the respondents felt that the most significant impact of the current work force shortage is on the existing information security work force. Finally, the greatest area of need for additional training and certification is in cloud computing. We need to fill that gap as soon as possible to ensure that we don't face burnout and departure from the current work force. And we need to get training programs in place in key priority areas like cloud security.

Let me now turn to women in the cyber work force. As stated earlier, we strongly support bringing more gender and ethnic diversity into the cyber work force. It is a key to helping close the growing gap that we face in both the public and private sectors here in the United States. For this particular segment we partnered with the Executive Women's Forum on Information Security, Risk Management, and Privacy. As the overall report shows, the work force gap continues to rise. Globally, the number of women professionals in the field remains stagnant at 11% (14% for North America). While this is extremely low, it is higher than in Europe or Asia, both of which are in single digits. The report also shows that women continue to lag behind when it comes to pay equity, despite higher levels of education. The report found that more than half of women respondents have faced discrimination in the workplace. Globally, men are four times more likely to attain C-level and Executive-level positions and nine times more likely to hold managerial positions in the cybersecurity field. On the positive side, women do feel more valued when participating in mentorship, sponsorship, and leadership development programs.

We believe that focusing on fixing the above-mentioned areas—pay inequity, creating a more inclusive workplace, valuing education, and providing mentorship and development opportunities for women to advance—can move the needle in the right direction and help bring more women into the cyber work force.

In conclusion, demand for cyber workers continues to grow. Unfortunately, the current work force gap is also growing. We must work together—Government, training and certification organizations, educational institutions and the private sector— to help close that gap.

Cybersecurity is a critical component of our National security. And the key factor to ensuring a more secure IT infrastructure is a skilled and trained cyber work force. As I highlighted in the data from the 2017 Global Information Security Workforce Study, we have many challenges ahead of us. However, this study also points us to solutions such as training and certification, bringing diversity into the work force and through leadership development and mentorship, and finally through incentives and pay equity.

I would like to request that the Global Information Security Workforce Study and the accompanying segments on Government and women be included in the record. Again, on behalf of (ISC)² and its 125,000 members, I thank you for the opportunity to provide our input. Thank you again for your focus on the cyber work force. We look forward to continuing to be a resource to the committee and to working with the subcommittee on this critical National security issue.

Mr. RICHMOND. I would also ask unanimous consent that Ms. Barragán be allowed to participate in today's hearing.

Mr. RATCLIFFE. Welcome.

Mr. RICHMOND. Thank you, Mr. Chairman. I yield back.

[The statement of Mr. Richmond follows:]

STATEMENT OF RANKING MEMBER CEDRIC L. RICHMOND

SEPTEMBER 7, 2017

For some time now, experts have predicted that the demand for cybersecurity professionals was quickly outpacing supply. In 2012, the Bureau of Labor Statistics projected that by 2020, there would be 400,000 computer scientists available to fill 1.4 million computer science jobs. Recent estimates suggest the deficit is growing instead of shrinking, and may reach 1.8 million by 2022.

Let's be clear—this is nothing short of a threat to National security. These are the professionals we rely on to help us prepare for and respond to the next WannaCry, Marai, or Fancy Bear. These are the people who will prevent state-sponsored hackers from taking down our electrical grid or infiltrating our State election systems.

And these are the experts we need to stand on the front lines during a major cyber attack and make sure we have functioning hospitals, banks, transportation systems, and lines of communication.

We need cybersecurity professionals in the private sector protecting our intellectual property and personal data, and we need them in the public sector protecting our Nation's most sensitive intelligence. Yet, we know that the Federal Government—and DHS in particular—is struggling to compete with the private sector for cyber talent.

What's more, this administration has failed to fill even the most critical, senior-level cybersecurity posts—asking agencies like DHS's National Programs and Protection Directorate to carry out broad, complex cybersecurity missions without a permanent under secretary. This lack of leadership makes us vulnerable. We should be doing everything we can to "right-size" our cybersecurity labor force—and there's a lot more we can do.

We need to introduce students to computers before they get to college—even the ones who go to schools that can't afford expensive tech programs and specialist instructors. I also believe there may be untapped potential in vocational schools, 2-year programs, and minority-serving institutions.

And once we've figured out how to get more people to choose cybersecurity as a career, we need to convince them to turn down a higher-paying job and spend some time in Federal service. Within the Federal Government, we need to promote recruitment and retention programs, particularly at DHS, which has lagged behind other cyber-focused Federal agencies like the NSA or FBI in attracting cyber talent.

For its part, DHS needs to be more forward-thinking and learn to anticipate the needs of an evolving work force that values professional development, a flexible work culture, and the ability to transition in and out of positions or even fields.

In closing, there is no question that the cyber work force challenge is a daunting one—but the stakes are too high to ignore it. Last year, the global economy lost over $450 billion to cyber criminals—and over 2 billion personal records were stolen in the United States alone. Meanwhile, studies show that less than half of U.S. businesses would say they are prepared for a cyber attack, and small "Main Street" businesses are struggling the most.

I look forward to hearing the testimony of our witnesses today, and hope we can identify innovative ways to work together to address cybersecurity work force challenges.

Mr. RATCLIFFE. Other Members of the committee are reminded that opening statements may be submitted for the record.

[The statement of Ranking Member Thompson follows:]

STATEMENT OF RANKING MEMBER BENNIE G. THOMPSON

SEPTEMBER 7, 2017

Good afternoon. I would like to thank Chairman Ratcliffe and Ranking Member Richmond for holding today's hearing to continue the work of identifying solutions to an on-going National challenge: The cyber work force shortage.

I want to take this opportunity to express my growing concern about the number of cybersecurity leadership vacancies across the Federal Government.

There are numerous vacancies in cybersecurity positions across the Executive Branch, and last month, 8 of the 28 members of the National Infrastructure Advisory Council resigned in protest of the President's failure to prioritize cybersecurity.

Most dramatically, this administration has chased out the State Department's first cybersecurity coordinator and plans to bury the State Department's cyber office in the Office of Bureau of Economic and Business Affairs.

And as we speak, there has been no nomination of someone to serve as the under secretary of the Department of Homeland Security's National Protection and Programs Directorate, which is tasked with leading the Federal Government's efforts to secure our Nation's critical infrastructure and protect Federal civilian networks from malicious cyber activity.

A strong cybersecurity posture is essential to National security and to our ability to compete in the global economy.

Policies necessary to build a strong cybersecurity posture require strong leadership.

I urge the President to quickly address cybersecurity leadership vacancies and organizational issues.

Turning to the issue at hand, I am eager to learn about innovative private-sector approaches to developing and maintaining the cybersecurity work force challenges.

I also hope to hear where the Federal Government can better partner with the private sector to cultivate the cybersecurity talent.

When I am in Mississippi, all too often, I get asked why so much focus is placed on importing cybersecurity talent from overseas instead of cultivating the talent we have here at home.

I support tech-visas, but at the same time agree with my constituents that we must more aggressively build and recruit a domestic cybersecurity work force.

We also must also do more to develop cybersecurity skills in overlooked talent pools.

Today, African Americans and Hispanics—combined—make up only 12 percent of the cybersecurity work force.

We need to do a better job understanding why that is.

We can and should continue expanding traditional career pathways to diverse populations—from building relationships between public and private-sector employers and diverse institutions of higher educations and implementing mentorship programs.

But we also have to start thinking "outside the box".

We need to get young people from all backgrounds interested in cybersecurity early and we need to figure out how to transition displaced employees into the cybersecurity work force.

According to Juniper Research, the cost of data breaches globally will increase to $2.1 trillion dollars by 2019.

And the State actors have demonstrated a clear interest in hacking into our critical infrastructure—from dams and the utility companies—to our elections.

We must build the cyber work force necessary to protect our National security and our economy.

Mr. RATCLIFFE. As I mentioned before, we are very pleased to have this distinguished panel of witnesses before us today on this vitally important topic. Dr. Frederick Chang is the executive director of the Darwin Deason Institute for Cyber Security at Southern Methodist University.

Dr. Chang, it is great to see you again and have a fellow Texan here today. Welcome.

Mr. CHANG. Thank you.

Mr. RATCLIFFE. Mr. Scott Montgomery is the vice president and chief technical strategist of McAfee.

We welcome you back to the subcommittee as well.

Dr. Michael Papay is the vice president and chief information security officer of Northrop Grumman.

Dr. Papay, it is always good to see you and thank you for being here today.

Finally, Ms. Juliet Okafor is the vice president of global business development of Fortress Information Security.

Ms. Okafor, welcome back to the subcommittee as well to you.

I would now ask all of the witnesses to stand and raise your right hand so I can swear you in to testify.

[Witnesses sworn.]

Please let the record reflect that each of the witnesses has been so sworn. You all may be seated.

The witnesses' full written statements will appear in the record. The Chair is now pleased to recognize Dr. Chang for 5 minutes for his opening remarks.

STATEMENT OF FREDERICK R. CHANG, EXECUTIVE DIREC-TOR, DARWIN DEASON INSTITUTE FOR CYBER SECURITY, SOUTHERN METHODIST UNIVERSITY

Mr. CHANG. Thank you. Chairman Ratcliffe, Ranking Member Richmond, Members of the subcommittee, thank you for the opportunity to appear before you today regarding the challenges associated with recruiting and retaining and cybersecurity work force.

My name is Frederick R. Chang and I am the executive director of the Darwin Deason Institute for Cyber Security at Southern Methodist University in Dallas, Texas. I am also the Bobby B. Lyle Centennial Distinguished Chair in Cybersecurity and professor in the Department of Computer Science and Engineering.

I don't need to reiterate to this group the nature of today's cyber threats and their consequences, so I will simply say that today's cyber insecurity is a multifaceted topic involving technology, policy, work force, and more. In my brief comments now, I will focus on the topic of work force.

One of the reasons why cyber compromises are so prevalent today is that there is a lack of trained and qualified personnel to defend the Nation's cyber assets. This lack of a trained cybersecurity work force has been referred to as the cyber skills gap. The gap is large and growing, as Chairman Ratcliffe and Ranking Member Richmond have both mentioned.

Hiring managers are having a hard time finding the talent they need right now and there is a critical need for technical talent. Organizations will get creative in their hiring practices. I believe the market will work in some very innovative ways to adapt to the changing conditions by, for example, retraining some workers for roles in cyber and moving them around to manage the workload.

Talent can and will come from some unexpected places. I am sure we will hear some creative ideas from the other panelists.

But the fact that the problem is growing is a serious issue because there have been a number of important activities that have been on-going for a while now around the country in academia, in industry and in Government. I will quickly touch on just a few of them now.

The NSA/DHS centers of academic excellence, the DOD and NSF cyber scholarship programs have been good and useful programs and have helped to jump-start and bolster university cybersecurity programs around the country. As universities grow their cyber portfolios to train more students, they will benefit from comprehensive curricular guidance and important progress is being made on that front.

Student cyber competitions are becoming increasingly popular. As long as we can ensure the right balance between the competitions and coursework, I am a supporter of these competitions because I think they build depth of knowledge and they provide a valuable team experience which will be useful when the students enter the work force.

We are also seeing now more cyber summer camps for both middle and high school students. I think these summer camps are quite important because they will help us grow a pool of cyber- and STEM-, science-, technology-, engineering-, and math-motivated students. We need a larger pipeline of folks from which to recruit into key cyber positions.

We will also see an increasing effort to advance technologies that will help automate different cybersecurity tasks and this will assist in giving human cyber experts more time to perform other tasks that we will not be able to automate at the time.

Let me close by saying that, in general, the actions that are being taken now are important, valuable, and are making a difference. But given that these actions are being taken and the fact that the cyber skills gap continues to grow tells me that we must do more.

In 1958, science education in America got a shot in the arm when the National Defense Education Act was passed the year after the Soviet satellite Sputnik was launched into outer space. This act helped launch a generation of students who would study math and science. So while we need to work very hard today to recruit and retain urgent cyber positions today and in the near future, I hope we can also consider the future of cyber space.

How secure will it be? How will we defend it? Today's students will be responsible for designing, creating, operating, maintaining, and defending tomorrow's cyber infrastructure. We need a large and capable pool of folks to staff these positions for the future.

Thank you again for allowing me to be here today. I look forward to your questions.

[The prepared statement of Dr. Chang follows:]

PREPARED STATEMENT OF FREDERICK R. CHANG

SEPTEMBER 7, 2017

Chairman Ratcliffe, Ranking Member Richmond, Members of the subcommittee, thank you for the opportunity to testify before you in today's hearing regarding the challenges associated with recruiting and retaining a cybersecurity work force. My name is Frederick R. Chang and I consider it an honor and a privilege to come before this subcommittee. I am the executive director of the Darwin Deason Institute for Cyber Security at Southern Methodist University (SMU) in Dallas, Texas. I am also the Bobby B. Lyle Centennial Distinguished Chair in Cyber Security, Professor in the Department of Computer Science and Engineering in SMU's Lyle School of Engineering, and a senior fellow in SMU's John G. Tower Center for Political Studies. Prior to coming to SMU, I have held academic positions at the University of Texas at San Antonio and at the University of Texas at Austin. I have worked in the private sector and have also served as the director of research at the National Security Agency. I would also mention that I served as a member of the CSIS Commission on Cybersecurity for the 44th Presidency.

SMU is a Nationally-ranked private university in Dallas founded over 100 years ago. The university enrolls more than 11,000 students—including about 5,200 graduate students—who all benefit from the academic opportunities and international reach of seven degree-granting schools. The Carnegie Foundation recognizes SMU as a university with "high research activity," which ranges across disciplines from particle physics at the Large Hadron Collider at CERN, to geothermal energy, to the science of human speed, to cybersecurity through the Bobby B. Lyle School of Engineering. SMU's Lyle School of Engineering, founded in 1925, is one of the oldest engineering schools in the Southwest. The school offers eight undergraduate and 29 graduate programs, including master's and doctoral degrees, through the departments of Civil and Environmental Engineering; Computer Science and Engineering; Electrical Engineering; Engineering Management, Information, and Systems; and Mechanical Engineering. Finally, the Darwin Deason Institute for Cyber Security is a research institute with the goal of advancing the science, policy, application and education of cybersecurity through basic and problem-driven, interdisciplinary research.

THE NEW NORMAL

Early computer worms and viruses date back to the 1970's and 80's and while they were rare and experimental back then, as we fast forward to 2017, terms such as "malware", "data breach", "phishing" and "botnets" are unfortunately all too common today. We are no longer surprised to read about the latest data compromise or cyber attack as they are sadly a regular occurrence. In fact, not long ago a technology company ran a series of television commercials depicting that it is newsworthy when there is not a data breach. The internet, high-performance computing clusters, high-density storage, ultra high-speed communication links, the cloud, our laptops, and smart phones are technologies that we take for granted today. They are so integral to our personal and professional lives that it is hard to remember a time when we didn't have these technologies available to us. But in the larger scheme of things the technologies that comprise cyber space are young and changing at a stunning rate of speed. As we have become increasingly dependent on these technologies we have also come to understand just how vulnerable these technologies are to malicious attackers of many kinds. We have also come to understand the consequences of these security vulnerabilities to us personally, professionally, and to our National security.

The source of today's cyber insecurity is multifaceted, involving technology, policy, law, economics, work force, and more. In my brief comments this afternoon, I will focus on the topic of today's hearing: The cybersecurity work force. One of the reasons why cyber intrusions are so prevalent today is that there is a lack of trained, qualified personnel to defend the Nation's cyber assets. This lack of trained personnel has been referred to as the "cyber skills gap".

THE CYBER SKILLS GAP

Over the past several years there has been increasing concern about the cyber skills gap problem, and the extent to which this gap contributes to the Nation's challenge in defending cyber space, today and into the future. An image that comes to mind is from the child's game of whack-a-mole. Cyber defenders within an enterprise are stretched too thin, quickly moving from issue to issue in an effort to keep their networks secure. Two natural questions to ask are: How large is the problem? Is the problem going to get worse in the future? There have been a number of studies and reports on this topic and I have listed a few illustrative bullets points below that shed some light on these questions. I would hasten to add that perhaps more important than the specific numbers that are listed are the trends that they suggest.

- The size of the global cyber skills gap was estimated at about 1 million people in a 2014 report.[1] [2]
- The size of cyber skills gap globally will grow to about 1.8 million in 2022. This is 20 percent higher than an estimate made 2 years earlier.[3]
- The size of the cyber skills gap in the United States was estimated to be over 200,000 in 2015.[4] The size of the cyber skills gap is estimated to grow to about 265,000 in North America by 2022.[3]
- In the United States there were nearly 300,000 on-line job listings for cybersecurity-related positions between April 2016 through March 2017, and the National average ratio of existing cybersecurity workers to cybersecurity job openings is only 2.5, while the National average for all jobs is 5.6 according to the website CyberSeek.[5]

In addition to the shortfall estimates above, it is instructive to look at some illustrative responses sampled from a variety of different surveys of different groups of cybersecurity professionals. The goal here is not to be exhaustive but rather to provide a perspective on some of the challenges facing enterprises as they address the challenges associated with hiring qualified cybersecurity workers.

In one international survey, the North American respondents reported that they were not able to fill open cybersecurity positions about 26 percent of the time and that for all respondents, over a quarter of the time finding an appropriate person for the job can take up to 6 months. In the same survey, respondents reported that while they do receive quite a few applicants for each job opening, most applicants are viewed as unqualified—and this response is reflected by the North American respondents to the survey as well.[6]

In another survey that included only North American respondents (Information Technology (IT), and IT security professionals), 35 percent reported that there is a shortage of IT security professionals at most every level, and 37 percent reported that there are lots of less experienced/trained people, but it is hard to fill the most-skilled positions. In the same survey only 33 percent of respondents report that they have enough people to meet the threats they will face in the coming year and only 23 percent report that their security team is well-trained and up-to-date on the latest technologies and threats.[7]

In a study we conducted at SMU we explored how organizations made cybersecurity investment decisions.[8] We conducted semi-structured interviews with cybersecurity executives and managers from primarily four vertical sectors: Health care, financial, retail, and Government. Over 75 percent of the respondents were from U.S. organizations. Consistent with the findings reported above, our respondents reported that finding qualified cybersecurity talent was a key challenge. Sufficient budgets were often available for a particular cybersecurity project but that lack of availability of qualified personnel served as a limiting factor in budget requests. Respondents reflected that even though they had considerable professional networks from which to draw, they had difficulty finding the talent they needed.

Finally, a theme that was highlighted in one of the earlier reports on the cyber skills gap emphasized the need for technical talent. Indeed this need is reflected in the report title: *A Human Capital Crisis in Cybersecurity: Technical Proficiency Matters.*[9] A quote from the report describes the sentiment well: "We not only have a shortage of the highly technically skilled people required to operate and support systems we have already deployed; we also face an even more desperate shortage of people who can design secure systems, write safe computer code, and create the ever more sophisticated tools needed to prevent, detect, mitigate, and reconstitute systems after an attack".

---

[1] Cisco 2014 Annual Security Report, Cisco Systems, San Jose, CA, 2014.

[2] Cobb, S. Sizing the Cybersecurity Skills Gap: A White Paper, 2016. Paper can be found here: *http://cisosurvey.org/wp-content/uploads/2016/10/sizing-cyber-skills-gap-v1a.pdf.*

[3] 2017 Global Information Security Workforce Study: Benchmarking Workforce Capacity and Response to Cyber Risk, report can be found here: *https://iamcybersafe.org/wp-content/uploads/2017/07/N-America-GISWS-Report.pdf.*

[4] Setalvad, A. Demand to fill cybersecurity jobs booming, Peninsula Press, March 31, 2015, report can be found here: *http://peninsulapress.com/2015/03/31/cybersecurity-jobs-growth/.*

[5] *http://cyberseek.org/heatmap.html.*

[6] State of Cyber Security 2017, Part 1: Current Trends in Workforce Development, ISACA, 2017.

[7] Chickowski, E. Surviving the IT Security Skills Shortage, Dark Reading Reports, May 2017.

[8] Moore, T., Dynes, S. & Chang, F. Identifying How Firms Manage Cybersecurity Investment. Paper presented at the 15th Annual Workshop on the Economics of Information Security, June 13–14, 2016 Berkeley, California.

[9] A Human Capital Crisis in Cybersecurity: Technical Proficiency Matters. A White Paper of the CSIS Commission on Cybersecurity for the 44th Presidency, July 2010.

CYBER STUDENTS IN DEMAND

The previous section provided some perspective on the size and nature of the cyber skills gap today and into the future and the trends are that the gap is large and challenging today and that it will worsen in the years ahead. As enterprises think through how they will staff to meet their cyber defense needs they will do well to think creatively and unconventionally as talent could well come from disciplines that are not traditionally associated with cybersecurity. Additionally, as cybersecurity becomes a higher priority within an enterprise, talented employees from different parts of the enterprise can and are being retrained to move into higher-priority cyber positions. In fact, we've offered an MS degree in Security Engineering for over a decade at SMU and that degree is popular with corporate employees who are interested in retraining themselves.

For an enterprise it is clearly desirable to be able to hire highly-experienced professionals who can immediately perform at a high level, but due to the talent shortage and associated salary limitations that may not always be possible. An alternate strategy may be to strategically hire more junior talent and patiently grow the needed capability internally. Indeed in our own research [8] some of our respondents expressed this perspective. So, in addition to the natural course of hiring college graduates for positions that are appropriate for their skill level, there is additional demand for cyber-capable college graduates. I am seeing this demand for our students at SMU as are my peers around the country for their students at their respective universities.

As part of our undergraduate computer science major, we've offered a security track for many years now in which students can take elective courses in security which allows them to emphasize cybersecurity as part of their undergraduate computer science major. We are seeing an uptick in the number of students who are pursuing this security track and we believe that when students pursue this track they very often go on to pursue a cybersecurity-related job upon graduation. In addition, anecdotally, we are seeing an uptick in the number of high-school seniors who plan to pursue cybersecurity in their undergraduate studies.

ANSWERING THE NEED

The cyber skills gap has been known about and discussed for many years now and over time, I've had my fair share of discussions with enterprise managers who are eagerly awaiting the arrival of more trained cyber defenders. As mentioned above these students are in high demand. While for many hiring managers the supply of students isn't arriving fast enough to meet the demand, there are many activities underway in the government, the private sector, and academia—often working together—that are helping to meet the demand. Let me touch on a few such activities below.

Centers of Academic Excellence and Scholarships.—Historically the NSA/DHS Centers of Academic Excellence in Cyber Defense (CAE–CD) program (and extensions) have helped to jump start skill building in cybersecurity in higher education, by among other things, requiring the CAE–CD-designated universities to map their curriculum to specific information assurance knowledge units. Additionally the Government has funded scholarship programs (the NSF CyberCorps® Scholarship for Service, and the Department of Defense, Information Assurance Scholarship Program) that have provided funding (tuition, books, stipend, etc.) for students to complete their cybersecurity education in return for service to the Government following graduation.

Curricular guidance.—As more university capability, capacity, and programs are created to answer the need for more cyber defenders it will be important to have clear curricular guidelines that will assist in building these new programs. Cybersecurity is still a young field but is emerging as a distinct discipline. As universities compose new cybersecurity academic programs out of elements from computer science, computer engineering, information systems and the like, it will be extremely valuable to have comprehensive curricular guidance. The ACM (Association for Computing Machinery) Joint Task Force on Cybersecurity Education is in the process of creating this guidance and it is expected to be released later this year. [10] Importantly it defines cybersecurity as an interdisciplinary area of study including elements from risk management, policy, human factors, law and more, but that fundamentally is a computing-based discipline.

Cyber Competitions.—For over a decade now university students have been competing in a cybersecurity competition that is now known as the National Collegiate

---

[8] See note, previous page.
[10] *https://www.csec2017.org/*.

Cyber Defense Competition (NCCDC). The competition provides a challenging and motivating event in which students must defend a simulated small company network while operationally keeping services up and running while responding to business requests. Depending on how they do, points are scored and teams advance in the competition. The competition has grown in popularity over the years and now there are 10 regions across the country that compete, and the regional winners compete in a National finals event. At the National finals event, a National winner is crowned. Cyber competitions in general have become very popular, and there are now many in which to participate and they focus in different areas (cybersecurity, forensics, and capture-the-flag). With the increasing number of cyber competitions it is fair to ask about their educational impact.[11] That said, cyber competitions provide a means to increase depth of technical knowledge in cybersecurity[12] and there is some evidence that cyber competitions will attract individuals who will stay in the field a long time.[13] At SMU there is a student-run security club where interested students meet to learn from each other and practice security concepts. A highlight for club members is to participate in cyber competitions including the NCCDC. The cyber competitions are popular with the students in part because they feel the competitions provide a valuable supplement to what they learn in class. Additionally, cyber competitions give students experience working as part of a team, and this is valuable when they graduate and join the work force. As the popularity of cyber competitions has continued to grow, they have moved into the K–12 domain as well.

Cyber summer camps.—Related to, but distinct from cyber competitions, are summer cybersecurity camps for K–12 students. For example, the GenCyber program, funded by NSA and NSF, offers a summer cybersecurity camp experience to middle and high school students, as well as teachers, in an effort to increase the pool of students who might go on to study cybersecurity in the United States. One of the goals of these summer camps is to teach students about cyber safe and correct online behaviors. Over the last several years, in keeping with the effort to get more K–12 students interested in the STEM (Science, Technology, Engineering, and Math) fields, among other things, SMU has conducted a Crime Scene Investigation (CSI) summer camp for middle schoolers. Students are introduced to the science, technology, and math behind CSI via expert presentations from real-world professionals and hands-on activities. For the past two summers we have added a cybersecurity module into the CSI curriculum.

Augmenting human capability with technology.—Finally, there are some important efforts to augment human capability in cybersecurity via the use of technology. For example, there is promise in the use of advanced reasoning techniques to augment the human cyber expert by automating some portions of the cyber defense task (e.g., finding and fixing flaws in software). This was the goal of the recent DARPA Cyber Grand Challenge in which important advances were made in the ability to automate the process of detecting software vulnerabilities, creating an appropriate patch, and then applying that patch in real-time.[14] To the extent that these, and other, difficult and time-consuming tasks can be automated, this will leave the time-limited human cyber expert more time to perform important analytic tasks that are not able to be automated at this time.

CONCLUSIONS

Many students I speak with are eager to join this new field and as mentioned previously we are seeing an uptick in that interest. I occasionally engage students in brief career-oriented discussions and a few themes emerge in these discussions as students think about their job choices that I thought might be relevant as we discuss recruiting and retaining top cyber talent.

1. The students want challenging work. They are challenged in their coursework to master difficult technical material, but also exercise creativity in using those skills. They want nothing less when they move into the workplace. They want to jump into the game and show that they have what it takes.

2. The students want to make a difference. As they evaluate positions they will try to determine if the position will allow them to make a difference—they want

---

[11] Fulton, S., Schweitzer, D., and Dressler, J. What Are We Teaching In Cyber Competitions? Frontiers in Education Conference (FIE), October 3–6, 2012.

[12] Manson, D., and Pike, R. The case for depth in cybersecurity education. ACM Inroads, Vol. 5, No. 1, pp. 47–52, March 2014.

[13] Tobey, D.H., Pusey, P., and Burley, D.L. Engaging learners in cybersecurity careers: lessons from the launch of the national cyber league, ACM Inroads, Vol. 5, No. 1, pp. 53–56, March 2014.

[14] *https://www.darpa.mil/news-events/2016–08–04.*

their efforts to have an impact. Sure, salary will be a factor, but as one student commented, for some they will choose "mission over money".

3. The students want to keep their technical skills sharp. When students graduate their technical skills are sharp and up-to-date. They understand that the computing and technological landscape changes rapidly. They will want to work with the most modern tools, with colleagues who they respect and from whom they can learn, and in an environment that gives them opportunities to refresh their technical skills.

In closing, in my comments earlier I briefly mentioned a number of activities that the Nation is undertaking now in an attempt to help close the cyber skills gap including: Scholarships, new cybersecurity curricular guidance, cyber competitions, cyber summer camps, and technological advances that will augment human cyber capability. These activities are important, valuable, and are making a difference, but I believe we can and should do more. We now have a much better understanding of the constantly-changing nature of the cyber threat and the consequences of our cyber insecurity. Are there lessons to be learned from America's "Sputnik moment" nearly 60 years ago? Following the launch of the Soviet satellite Sputnik in 1957, science education got an infusion of funds of over a billion dollars in 1958 when the National Defense Education Act was passed, and this helped launch a new generation of students who would to be motivated to go on to study math and science.[15] The challenge to make cyber space more secure is a long-term, enduring problem. While we urgently need short-term solutions to make available more cyber-trained workers to fill positions now and in the near-term, we also need to ask ourselves what will cyber space look like 10, 20, and 30 years from now—and how much more dependent will we be on it? Today's students will be responsible for designing, creating, operating, maintaining, and defending tomorrow's cyber infrastructure.

Mr. RATCLIFFE. Thank you, Dr. Chang.

The Chair now recognizes Mr. Montgomery for his opening statement.

STATEMENT OF SCOTT MONTGOMERY, VICE PRESIDENT AND CHIEF TECHNICAL STRATEGIST, MCAFEE

Mr. MONTGOMERY. Good afternoon, Chairman Ratcliffe, Ranking Member Richmond, and Members of the subcommittee. Thanks very much for the opportunity to testify today.

I am Scott Montgomery, vice president and chief technical strategist of McAfee, one of the world's leading independent cybersecurity companies.

Inspired by the power of working together, McAfee creates enterprise, Government, and consumer solutions that make the world a safer place.

As a group, we have studied this well-documented work force shortage for several years now and we need to do something about it immediately. Following are some recommendations for training and incentivizing more people and also using technology to help fill the gap.

First, we should expand programs that are working today, such as the NSF CyberCorps Scholarship for Service Program which manages to retain an impressive 80 percent of its graduates as workers for the Federal Government. We should also consider expanding this program to focus on community colleges. These institutions tend to attract a diverse variety of students, including recent high school grads, but also returning veterans and other adult students who might be working full or part time.

---

[15] Abramson, L. Sputnik Left Legacy for U.S. Science Education, All Things Considered, NPR, September 30, 2007. Story can be found here: *http://www.npr.org/templates/story/story.php?storyId=14829195*.

I want to recognize full committee Chairman McCaul's Cyber Scholarship Opportunities Act and its Senate counterpart that was recently voted out of committee. Both require the NSF program to include students pursuing an associate's degree in cybersecurity without the intent of transferring to a 4-year institution.

The public sector as well as the private sector have thorny challenges in attracting and retaining cybersecurity talent. At the very high level, there are three categories of Government cyber professionals. There are operators, the people who implement and keep security technology running, researchers who explore the latest in cyber defense, and finally analysts, experts that can respond to an event in the first few minutes. It is this third area where Government and the private sector have the most serious need.

Congress gave DHS expedited hiring authority for cybersecurity 3 years ago, an authority that could address many of the suggestions. It is incumbent upon the Department not only to move these plans forward, but also to come up with creative ways to address the known pay disparity between the public sector and the private sector. Whether this is through accelerated grades or accelerated retirement packages, there has to be some creative way where we can address the pay disparity.

We should also explore creative ways to enable the public and private sectors to share talent. Adversaries are constantly innovating and changing course. It is unrealistic to think that Government cyber practitioners will be able to keep up with a rapidly-evolving environment by themselves.

We should design a mechanism for cyber professionals to move back and forth between the public and private sector so that the Government organizations would have a continual refresh of expertise, much like the National Guard.

We should work quickly to solve this cyber work force challenge. But in the mean time, while we still have this gap, we must rely on technology, such as moving to the cloud and using automation wisely. We can automate lower-level tasks, freeing up personnel to serve in key roles that humans can best fill. Those are the analysts who can use creative insight to determine why an attacker might have chosen a particular attack method or target or how best to respond to an incident.

When considering the role of security technologies, it is important to understand the market-like forces that drive the effectiveness of cybersecurity defense. Information technologies continuously improve over time.

Paradoxically, cyber defense do not follow this pattern. Their effectiveness peaks shortly after release and degrades quickly thereafter. When a new defensive capability is first released, adversaries don't take much notice. But once it is deployed at scale, they adopt evasion tactics and countermeasures causing the effectiveness to degrade significantly.

We also see the current paradigm of constant integration of point products as ineffective and unsustainable, particularly given the substantial number of cyber professionals needed to knit together these disparate systems. Not only are technology efficiencies already declining by the time the lengthy acquisition and deployment cycles are complete, but organizations are unable to deal with the complexity of what they have acquired and deployed.

An approach where technology enabled with strong collaboration can be deployed rapidly to security platforms using open-source communication means as required. Both the public and private-sector organizations need their tools to utilize these kinds of open-source communication mechanisms.

No single industry partner can cover the vast spectrum of security and privacy problems or catch every issue every time. Only by working collaboratively in the private and public sectors can we defeat cyber attackers.

I look forward to our discussion and would be happy to answer any questions. Thank you.

[The prepared statement of Mr. Montgomery follows:]

PREPARED STATEMENT OF SCOTT MONTGOMERY

SEPTEMBER 7, 2017

Good afternoon, Chairman Ratcliffe, Ranking Member Richmond, and Members of the subcommittee. Thank you for the opportunity to testify today. I am Scott Montgomery, vice president and chief technical strategist of McAfee, LLC.

I am pleased to address the subcommittee on the challenges of recruiting and retaining a cybersecurity work force. My testimony will address the broad contours of the cybersecurity skills shortage, both in the public and private sectors, and what we can do about it. One involves people: Training more, broadening our perception of what attributes and skills are needed, and incentivizing Government investments in cyber specialists. The other involves technology: Moving to the cloud, using automation wisely, and encouraging industry to move to interoperable platforms.

First, I would like to provide some background on my experience and McAfee's commitment to cybersecurity. I help drive the company's technical innovation, evangelize our expertise, thought leadership, and offerings to public and individual audiences; and work to increase the public trust by cooperating with law enforcement on cyber criminal investigations and disruption. With more than 20 years in content and network security, I bring a practitioner's perspective to the art and science of cybersecurity. I have designed, built, tested, and certified information security and privacy solutions for such companies as McAfee, Secure Computing, and on behalf of a wide variety of public-sector organizations.

MCAFEE'S COMMITMENT TO CYBERSECURITY

McAfee is one of the world's leading independent cybersecurity companies. Inspired by the power of working together, McAfee creates business and consumer solutions that make the world a safer place. By building solutions that work with other industry products, McAfee helps businesses orchestrate cyber environments that are truly integrated, where protection, detection, and correction of threats happen simultaneously and collaboratively. By protecting consumers across all their devices, we secure their digital lifestyle at home and away. By working with other security players, we are leading the effort to unite against State-sponsored actors, cyber criminals, hacktivists, and other disruptors for the benefit of all.

THE CYBERSECURITY SKILLS GAP

In 2016 the Center for Strategic and International Studies (CSIS) and McAfee undertook a study titled *Hacking the Skills Shortage* based on a global survey of IT professionals. Some of the findings about the cybersecurity talent gap include:
- 82 percent of those surveyed reported a lack of cybersecurity skills within their organization.
- 71 percent agreed that the talent shortfall makes organizations more vulnerable to attackers, and 25 percent say that lack of sufficient cybersecurity staff has actually contributed to data loss or theft and reputational damage.
- The most desirable skills cited in all 8 countries surveyed were intrusion detection, secure software development, and attack mitigation.
- 76 percent of respondents say their governments are not investing enough in programs to help cultivate cybersecurity talent and believe the laws and regulations for cybersecurity in their country are inadequate.

Since that July study, the numbers haven't improved any. According to a recent *Global Information Security Workforce Study*, the cybersecurity work force shortage is projected to reach 1.8 million by 2022. The cybersecurity skills shortage is equally troublesome in the Federal Government. Tony Scott, the Federal Government's former CIO, said in a GovLoop article, "There are an estimated 10,000 openings in the Federal Government for cyber professionals that we would love to fill, but there's just not the talent available." Given the vital role such Government agencies as the Departments of Defense and Homeland Security as well as the intelligence agencies play in protecting the United States, this skills gap is disquieting and merits attention from policy makers.

None of this is news. We've studied this work force shortage for several years now, and if we're serious about its importance we need to do something about it immediately. Following are some recommendations for training and incentivizing more people and also using technology to help fill the gap.

TRAIN AND CROSS-TRAIN MORE PEOPLE

Expand the Current CyberCorps Program

First, we need to focus on expanding existing programs that train people in the cybersecurity field. For example, The CyberCorps Scholarship for Service (SFS) program is designed to increase and strengthen the cadre of Federal information assurance specialists that protect Government systems and networks. The program is structured so that The National Science Foundation (NSF) provides grants to about 70 institutions across the country to offer scholarships to 10–12 full-time students each. With this structure, students get free tuition for up to 2 years in addition to annul stipends—$22,500 for undergraduates and $34,000 for graduate students. They also get allowances for health insurance, textbooks, and professional development. Some universities also partner with the Department of Homeland Security (DHS) on these programs.

Generally, students must be juniors or seniors and must qualify for the program by attaining a specific GPA, usually at least a 3.0 or higher. Upon completing their coursework and a required internship, students earn a degree, then go to work as security experts in a Government agency for at least the amount of time they have been supported by the program. After that, they can apply for jobs in the public or private sector.

With additional funding, the CyberCorps SFS program could be expanded to more institutions and more students within each of those schools. To date, the Federal Government has made a solid commitment to supporting the SFS program, having spent $45 million in 2015, $50 million in 2016, and the most recent administration's budget requesting $70 million. As a baseline, an investment of $40 million pays for roughly 1,500+ students to complete the scholarship program.

With the cyber skills deficit being substantial, policy makers should significantly increase the size of the program, possibly something in the range of $180 million. If this level of funding were appropriated, the program could support roughly 6,400 scholarships. This investment would make a dent in the Federal cyber skills deficit, estimated to be in the range of 10,000 per year. At the same time, this level of investment could help create a new generation of Federal cyber professionals who could serve as positive role models for a countless number of middle and high school students across the country to consider the benefits of a cyber career and Federal service. On a long-term scale, this positive feedback loop of the SFS program might be its biggest contribution.

Create a Community College Program

While the CyberCorps program serves college juniors and seniors who are already well along the learning path, we believe another program, or an expansion of the SFS program, could seek to attract high school graduates who don't yet have specific career aspirations. Private companies could partner with a community college in their area to establish a course of study focusing on cybersecurity. The Federal Government could fund all or part of the tuition remission for students. Interested students would be taught both by college faculty and private-sector practitioners. For example, an IT company could offer several faculty members/guest lecturers who would participate during a semester. Students would receive free tuition—paid by a Federal program, perhaps with private-sector contributions—but they would not receive a stipend for living arrangements, as 4-year college students do in the CyberCorps program. Students would receive a 2-year certificate in cybersecurity that would be transferrable to a 4-year school. Like the CyberCorps program, graduates would spend the same amount of time as their scholarship period, working in a guaranteed Government job.

Community colleges tend to attract a variety of students—including recent high school graduates but also returning veterans and other adult students who might have pursued other careers or might even be working full- or part-time. The community college option could also further ethnic and racial diversity in a cyber program—something that is badly needed. This diversity would be a plus rather than a minus for the cybersecurity profession, as the field requires a diverse set of skills and individuals. Not all of these skills are strictly technical, and for those that are technical, not all require high levels of formal education. You don't need a Ph.D.—or even a bachelor's degree—to work in cybersecurity. For instance, a 4-year degree is not necessarily required to work in a security operations center (SOC). As pointed out earlier, a strong security operation requires various levels of skills, and having a flexible scholarship program at a community college could benefit a wide variety of applicants while providing the profession with other types of necessary skills.

Encourage Cultural Changes to Close the Cyber Skills Gap

As cybersecurity is one of the greatest technical challenges of our time, we need to be creative in attracting more people to the work force. One of the ways we can do this is by changing our way of thinking about the industry. Cybersecurity professionals can—and do—have broad and varied backgrounds. Diverse skills and experience can enable them to examine problems from a different perspective, bringing creativity rather than just linear thinking to cyber problems and solutions. The legacy tech innovator Bell Labs proved that diverse teams produce more creative, high-quality products. Likewise, a diverse incident response team can benefit from look at cyber incidents and responses from a multitude of perspectives.

We must also address the gender and diversity gap, which would help alleviate the skills gap. In North America, women constitute only 14 percent of the information security work force, according to a Women in Cybersecurity report by the Executive Women's Forum and (ISC). The numbers are even worse for African Americans, who comprise only 3 percent of information security analysts in the United States, according to the Bureau of Labor Statistics figures cited in an article in *Forbes*. Research on large, innovative organizations has shown that gender and racial diversity improves the organizations' financial performance. The title of this article in *Scientific American* states the case well: How Diversity Makes Us Smarter: Being around people who are different from us makes us more creative, more diligent and harder working. McAfee believes we need to focus on hiring a diverse work force, which will in turn make us an even stronger company.

Pass Legislation like the "Cyber Scholarship Opportunities Act of 2017"

I'd also like to take a moment to applaud the recently approved "Cyber Scholarship Opportunities Act of 2017" that was passed through the Senate Commerce, Science, and Transportation Committee, as well as Chairman McCaul's "Cyber Scholarship Opportunities Act of 2017." Both bills require the SFS program to include students pursuing an associate's degree in a cybersecurity field without the intent of transferring to a bachelor's degree program, people who have a bachelor's degree already, or people who are veterans of the Armed Forces.

This is encouraging news for closing the skills gap at the operator and junior analyst levels. McAfee supports these bills and hopes they get signed into law. However, there is still more work to be done. The Senate bill directs the NSF to provide awards to improve cybersecurity education and increase teacher recruitment. We hope the Senate considers those with hands-on cybersecurity experience as potential candidates for teaching.

The Thorny Problem of the Government's Gap

The cybersecurity skills gap also extends to Government. Quite simply, the public sector can't keep up with the private sector in terms of pay scale and benefits. We have to change that to be able to attract and retain excellent cyber professionals in the public sector. To date, the SFS program has been particularly effective in adding to cybersecurity talent in the Government. While all graduates are required to begin their careers by serving in the Government, an impressive 70 percent, according to NSF, actually remain in Government jobs. I'd like to unpack this issue a bit and distinguish between different types of cyber professionals in Government organizations.

At a very high level, there are three categories of cyber professionals. First there are operators—the people who implement the security technology and keep it running in systems and networks. You don't need a Ph.D. in computer science to fill an operator role, and in fact the Government has a good supply of such people either directly or through contractors. Then there are researchers, people who explore the latest in cyber defense. Again, the Federal Government is well-served here by labs in the Department of Defense, DARPA, IARPA, and the intelligence community. The third category is analysts—the people who can respond to a breach in the first few minutes and conduct the necessary analytical work to understand the implications of an attack and develop a remediation plan. This is the area where the Government has the most serious need and where they need people who are not just technically trained but also astute and creative problem solvers.

In order to attract this kind of talent, the Federal Government needs to find ways to incentivize people and reduce obstacles to them serving in cybersecurity positions. The salary issue cannot be overlooked, as this is a major incentive for most professionals—especially in the most sought-after areas of IT like cybersecurity. Government needs to offer competitive salaries, and if that's not possible, Government should offer better retirement packages to be more on a par with the private sector. Alternatively, agencies could offer cybersecurity personnel the ability to up-level their positions (e.g., from a GS12 to a GS13) more quickly than usual.

Congress gave DHS expedited hiring authority for cybersecurity 3 years ago—an authority that could address many of these suggestions. It's incumbent upon the Department to move these plans forward as soon as possible.

Another impediment to getting cybersecurity personnel where they need to be in Government agencies has to do with clearances. Often an agency will require an advanced clearance to enter a facility when, in fact, many of the systems don't house Classified data. As there's a limited number of personnel with high-level security clearances—and as it takes a long while to get one—this also contributes to the cybersecurity talent shortage in Government. Expediting the vetting process and carefully reviewing which clearances are truly necessary to work on a system, while still protecting National security, would both be steps in the right direction.

Another topic that deserves attention is the need to review and declassify materials over time. This merits a lot more study, and I know there are efforts within the Defense Department, in particular, to better determine what data actually needs to be Classified and for how long. If data were to be declassified more quickly, more cybersecurity professionals with lower or no clearances would be able to be of service.

PUBLIC-PRIVATE SECTOR CROSS-POLLINATION

We must also develop creative approaches to enabling the public and private sectors to share talent, particularly during significant cybersecurity events. Cybersecurity is a rapidly changing area, and what's valid today might well be superseded tomorrow. We know that the adversary is constantly innovating and changing course, often reacting to new defensive capabilities the private sector develops. It's unrealistic to think that Government cyber practitioners would be able to keep up with such a rapidly-evolving environment without private-sector assistance. We should design a mechanism for cyber professionals—particularly analysts or those who are training to become analysts—to move back and forth between the public and private sector so that Government organizations would have a continual refresh of expertise.

One way to accomplish this would be for DHS to partner with companies and other organizations such as universities to staff a cadre of cybersecurity professionals—operators, analysts, and researchers—who are credentialed to move freely between public and private-sector service. These professionals, particularly those in the private sector, could be on call to help an impacted entity and the Government respond to a major hack in a timely way. Both Government and private-sector cybersecurity professionals would benefit from regular job rotations of possibly 2 to 3 weeks each year. This type of cross-pollination would help everyone share best practices on technology, business processes, and people management. DHS should include a flexible, public-private pool of certified professionals in its plan to rewrite its cybersecurity hiring and retention plan. If DHS is not ready to act, Congress should establish a blue-ribbon panel of public and private-sector experts to study how a flexible cadre of cybersecurity professionals could be started and managed. Much like the National Guard, a flexible staffing approach to closing the skills could become a model of excellence.

HOW TECHNOLOGY CAN HELP ALLEVIATE THE PROBLEM

Even though we should work hard and think creatively to fill it, the cyber skills gap won't be closed any time soon. In the mean time, we must rely technology more and more.

Moving to the Cloud

Both the Government and industry are moving their IT operations to the cloud. Last year, McAfee surveyed over 2,000 professionals for our annual cloud security research study, Building Trust in a Cloudy Sky: The State of Cloud Adoption and Security. We found that hybrid cloud adoption tripled in the last year, increasing from 19 percent to 57 percent in organizations surveyed. Additionally, IT executives believed their IT budget would be 80 percent cloud-based within an average of 13 months, and 73 percent of companies are planning to move to a fully software-defined data center within 2 years.

Here's the relevance to the work force shortage: As more organizations move to the cloud, the cloud providers rather than the organizations are delivering a baseline of foundational technology—hardware, operating systems, and so forth. This reduces the overall amount of labor that an organization's IT and information security staff needs to exert, leveraging cloud's inherent economies of scale. However, the move to the cloud will not, by itself, close the cyber skills gap in the short run; there are just too many open slots to fill. Indeed, our recent cloud study also found that 49 percent of businesses are currently delaying cloud deployment due to a cybersecurity skills gap. Nevertheless, the move to the cloud will help reduce the labor shortage; it will just take more time to pay off as more organizations off-load their IT environments to cloud providers.

Human-Machine Teaming

One strategy for addressing the cybersecurity skills deficit is to use automation—through such solutions as machine learning and artificial intelligence. Legacy IT systems, however—like many of those in the Federal Government—lack the ability to take advantage of the most contemporary security architectures and development techniques. While it is possible to isolate or wrap security around a legacy system, the approach is far inferior to a well-designed secure implementation designed for the security challenges of 2017 and beyond.

This speaks to the need for investments in IT modernization and modern cybersecurity solutions, which the President's Executive Order addresses. We support these much-needed policy changes, which will allow for better use of automation, or machine learning.

The ideal situation for now is what McAfee calls human-machine teaming. This means taking advantage of the particular strengths of each. Machine learning can save security teams both time and energy, as it is the fastest way to identify new attacks and push that information to endpoint security platforms. Machines are excellent at repetitive tasks, such as making calculations across broad swaths of data. That's one of the strengths of machine learning: Its ability to crunch big data sets and draw statistical inferences based on that data, detecting patterns hidden in the data at rapid speed.

Humans, on the other hand, are best at insight and analysis (the cybersecurity analysts referred to earlier). With the assistance of machine learning, human analysts can devise new defenses quickly, adapting to attackers' automated processes and limiting their effectiveness. The human intellect is capable of thinking like an adversary and understanding a scenario that might never have been executed in any environment previously. Machines can take over some simple processes, automating them so the humans can be free to understand context and implication, such as why a bad actor might want to attack a Government agency.

Fostering Interoperability

When considering the role of security technologies, it's important to understand the market-like forces that drive the effectiveness of cybersecurity defense. Most information technologies continuously improve over time. Paradoxically, cyber defense technologies do not follow this pattern. Their effectiveness peaks shortly after release and then degrades. When a new defensive capability is first released, bad actors take little notice, but once deployed at scale, they adopt evasion tactics and counter-measures, causing the effectiveness to significantly degrade.

Where does that leave us? We see the current paradigm of constant integration of point products—individual software applications—as ineffective and unsustainable, particularly given the substantial number of cyber professionals needed to knit together disparate systems. Not only are technology efficiencies already declining by the time the lengthy purchase and integration cycles are complete, but organizations are unable to deal with the complexity of supporting upwards of 30 or 40 independent tools and technologies. That's a losing game, but it's the one security practitioners find themselves playing.

We need a different approach where technology—enabled with strong collaboration—can be deployed rapidly to security platforms so they can communicate with each other over open communication protocols. Organizations in both the public and private sector need security tools that are interoperable and interchangeable to protect against existing and prospective threats. As cybersecurity solutions become interoperable, they become more efficient and cost-effective. They also become easier to maintain than a IT environment of disparate systems, the classic IT hair ball. Over time, more interoperable cybersecurity systems will contribute to closing the skills gap as they get more widely deployed. We call on the cybersecurity industry to design technology to an open standard, on an open platform, so customers are not locked into proprietary technologies that don't work with each other or allow for change.

McAfee has taken a major step toward fostering interoperability by opening our Data Exchange Layer (DXL)—a communications fabric that enables unprecedented collaboration in an open-source, real-time system—to other developers and vendors to use at no expense. OpenDXL—is at the core of our mission to enable security devices to share intelligence and orchestrate security operations at rapid speed. As of today, there are 13 companies connected to the DXL ecosystem, 12 others in testing or development, and 14 additional companies in the design phase.

OpenDXL is a big part of what we mean by Together Is Power. No single industry partner can cover the vast spectrum of security and privacy problems. No single industry partner will catch every issue every time. Only by working collaboratively in the private and public sectors can we defeat cyber attackers. This means bringing the best ideas, the best technologies and the best people to bear on our common security problem. It means leveraging technologies guided by the strategic intellect that only humans can provide. And to ensure that we have enough human intellect to work with our continually evolving technology, we need to encourage more people from diverse backgrounds to enter the cybersecurity field, train them, and—particularly in the case of Government—reward them.

I look forward to our discussion and will be happy to answer any questions.

Mr. RATCLIFFE. Thank you, Mr. Montgomery.

The Chair now recognizes Dr. Papay for 5 minutes for his opening remarks.

STATEMENT OF MICHAEL PAPAY, VICE PRESIDENT AND CHIEF INFORMATION SECURITY OFFICER, NORTHRUP GRUMMAN

Mr. PAPAY. Thank you, Chairman Ratcliffe, Ranking Member Richmond, and Members of the subcommittee for hosting today's important hearing.

As our Government, military, and society become increasingly dependent upon digital technology, it is a National and economic security imperative to ensure that we have a cyber-trained work force to meet this demand.

My name is Dr. Michael Papay and I am the vice president of cyber initiatives and the chief information security officer for Northrop Grumman, the leading cyber provider across the Federal Government.

As critical as technology is, at Northrop Grumman, we firmly believe that our employees are the single-most important aspect of cybersecurity, and we have made it a top priority to not only support the development of a larger cyber-qualified work force globally, but also to increase its diversity.

Like DHS and the Federal Government, Northrop Grumman can offer prospective employees something unique, the opportunity to do really exciting, cutting-edge work that is vital to our National security. For many cyber professionals, it is this sense of mission that drives them.

In 2012, I had the privilege of participating in the Homeland Security Advisory Council Task Force on Cyber Skills. I applaud DHS for adopting many of the task force recommendations, including additional cyber training which Northrop Grumman provided to hundreds of DHS employees. Northrop Grumman has also incorporated the majority of recommendations into our internal cyber work force strategy.

At Northrop Grumman, we look at the continuum of education from elementary school through the professional ranks to build a diverse, highly-skilled work force. The Northrop Grumman Foundation is honored to be the presenting sponsor of the Air Force Association's CyberPatriot Program, a youth, teen cyber defense competition which boasted over 4,400 teens from all 50 States last year. While most STEM programs report a female participation rate around 12 percent, I am especially proud that CyberPatriot boasts 23 percent female participation.

Northrop Grumman is actively engaged with universities across the country to help to develop curriculum, fund hands-on student research and development projects and educate future cyber professionals. Because cyber is such a complicated and dynamic challenge, we need a work force that brings with it a diversity of thought, culture, education, experience, and problem solving. Diversity drives innovation and breeds success.

Therefore, in many cases, we are specifically targeting investments to increase the participation of women and underrepresented groups in the cyber profession. For example, cyber scholars at the University of Maryland, Baltimore County, and the Cyber Warrior Diversity Program at Morgan State University and Coppin State University.

As part of our retention efforts and to support their growth, we rotate cyber professionals around the company to keep them engaged and challenged while also offering on-going educational and training opportunities. We even developed our own in-house cyber academy to provide our employees, customers, and even policy makers with the macro understanding and technical skills cyber often requires.

A few final thoughts to leave the committee with. On clearances, beyond just a shortage of cyber professionals, there is also a lack of cleared cyber professionals. We need to figure out ways to improve the clearance process to ensure that both the Federal Government and contractors have the cleared employees to do all the critical National security work that is required.

More cyber-trained Federal employees. Cyber training across the Federal Government is inconsistent. The Federal Government as a whole needs to put a greater emphasis on ensuring its employees have the cyber understanding and tools to effectively and securely do their jobs.

Increased partnerships and coordination. There is no single answer to addressing the shortage of cyber workers. Continuing to work across academia, Government, and industry is essential to leveraging investments, best practices, and collectively working together to ensure that our great Nation continues to securely grow and prosper in this increasingly digital age.

I would be happy to answer any questions. Northrop Grumman looks forward to working with the subcommittee on this effort. Thank you again.

[The prepared statement of Dr. Papay follows:]

PREPARED STATEMENT OF MICHAEL PAPAY

SEPTEMBER 7, 2017

Thank you Chairman Ratcliffe, Ranking Member Richmond, and Members of the House Homeland Security Subcommittee on Cybersecurity and Infrastructure Protection for holding today's hearing on the critical topics of attracting, retaining, educating, and training our Nation's cyber work force. As our Government, military, and society overall become increasingly dependent upon digital technology, it is a National AND economic security imperative to ensure that we have the cyber-trained work force to meet this demand.

My name is Dr. Michael Papay and I am vice president of cyber initiatives and chief information security officer (CISO) for Northrop Grumman, a leading cyber provider across the Federal Government and producer of innovative solutions from autonomous systems to strike platforms to space products. Given the often sensitive and critical National security nature of our work; it is absolutely essential for resilient cybersecurity to be a key component to all that we do. From original code, to hardware, to uninterrupted mission performance while enduring cyber threats, our customers trust us to deliver systems that enable them to confidently execute the mission in any environment, including cyber space. We are proud of our strong reputation earned through 70 years of integrity, innovation, dedication to the customer, and a proven track record of performance. As important as technology is, at Northrop Grumman we firmly believe that our employees are the single most important aspect of cybersecurity. Therefore, we have made it a top priority to not only support the development of a larger cyber qualified work force globally but also to increase its diversity.

Thank you again for having me here today and I hope that my testimony is useful. I look forward to your questions.

ATTRACTING AND RETAINING EMPLOYEES

Northrop Grumman is at the forefront of cyber research, development, and technology, and it is our people that make this possible. While Northrop Grumman, like the DHS and the Federal Government, must continue to work to overcome a perception hurdle for cyber talent—we can offer prospective employees something unique—the opportunity to do really exciting, cutting-edge work that is vital to our National security. For many cyber professionals (and employees across Northrop Grumman and the Federal Government) it is this sense of mission that drives them.

As part of our effort to ensure that our cyber employees are continually challenged and provided opportunities for growth, we move them around inside the company from customer to customer, tough problem to tough problem. We utilize rotational programs that expose and train our cyber work force in defending our network, enabling our customers' missions, and supporting full spectrum cyber operations. We work with employees to help them create their own growth along the cyber career path, give them the time to take the training necessary to maintain their certifications, and keep their knowledge and skills fresh. We even offer educational assistance in some instances.

To provide our employees, customers, and even policy makers with the macro understanding and technical skills cyber often requires, Northrop Grumman created its own, in-house "Cyber Academy". We also utilize a matrix model for customer mission support and employee development—allowing us to hire for critical skills and redeploy our talent across programs. We are committed to providing positions that work best for our employees by allowing flexible work schedules and opening up work locations in customer-approved non-traditional cyber hubs throughout the country to broaden our talent pool.

At Northrop Grumman, we are focused on attracting all those who are interested and qualify through a sense of mission, passion for solving complex challenges, and desire to work on cutting-edge technologies that they are unable to do anywhere else in the world.

PARTNERING WITH THE FEDERAL GOVERNMENT AND DHS CYBER TRAINING

In 2012, I had the privilege of participating in the Homeland Security Advisory Council Task Force on CyberSkills, an initiative that was launched to help develop a National security work force as well as enable DHS to recruit and retain its own cyber talent. I applaud DHS for adopting many of the Task Force's recommendations. At Northrop Grumman, I am pleased to note that we have incorporated the majority of these recommendations as part of our internal cyber work force strategy. Members of my team also participated in the DHS Cyber Education and Workforce

Development Working Group and then the NIST National Initiative for Cybersecurity Education (NICE). Northrop Grumman representatives are members of both the Collegiate Working Group and the K–12 Working Group. Our engagement brings industry perspective in full collaboration with Government and academia. We also contribute to the NIST NICE Workforce 2.0 model which creates a framework for professionalization of the cyber career.

Partnering with our Federal Government customers on cyber work force education and training is critical to supporting a National security mission and our mutual success. One of the key findings of the CyberSkills Task Force was the need to provide more cyber training to DHS employees and I am pleased that Northrop Grumman has helped support this initiative. Starting in 2014, as part of our National Cybersecurity & Communications Integration Center (NCCIC) contract, we began using 39 cyber training courses to help DHS employees increase their efficiency and improve retention. Our training program heavily leveraged our internal Northrop Grumman Cyber Academy for a large portion of the course content and developed a three-level competency model. Hundreds of DHS employees received targeted training ranging from how to review cyber threat analysis reports to effectively coordinating with partners. Northrop Grumman cyber practitioners provided advice and guidance on National-level cyber security policy as well as implementation and support of new or existing technical solutions to enhance the mission. These training plans aligned to Cyber Skills and Cyber Pay initiatives, with incentives tied to requisitions and future hirings.

NORTHROP GRUMMAN CYBER WORKFORCE DEVELOPMENT

Growing a cyber work force from the ground up begins with inspiring youth to pursue this field. At Northrop Grumman and for our customers, in working to build a cyber work force, we look at the continuum of education—from elementary school through the professional ranks—and are collaborating with academia and organizations world-wide to help address this issue and build a diverse, highly-skilled work force.

For more than 7 years—Northrop Grumman has partnered with the Air Force Association to present the CyberPatriot National Youth Cyber Education Program. CyberPatriot is one of our most successful and impactful initiatives and features the wildly popular annual cyber defense competition. It started in 2009 with 8 teams and I'm proud to say over 4,400 teams participated this past year from all 50 States, Canada, and Department of Defense Dependent Schools in the Pacific and Europe. Given the fact that teams average about 5 students, we are reaching tens of thousands of youth each year who are learning how to harden and protect computers and networks. A full 87 percent of CyberPatriot participants go on to pursue STEM degrees in college. In addition to deep technical skills, the students, through the program structure, their mentors and hands-on experience, also develop their talents in cyber ethics, collaboration, communication, and leadership—all life skills that enhance their career readiness. Northrop Grumman has awarded more than $350,000 in scholarships to winning teams. Like others in industry and Government, the company has employed these high school students as paid summer interns, more than 300 to date, working side-by-side with our cyber professionals. Many of these interns have stayed with Northrop Grumman, returning summer after summer for paid internships through high school and then college. While most STEM programs report a female participation rate around 12 percent, I am especially proud that CyberPatriot boasts 23 percent female participation! None of this could be accomplished without the academic partner of the program, the University of Texas San Antonio's Center for Infrastructure Assurance and Security. To that end, we have found that you cannot only focus on higher education or at the high school level. In many cases, students have already decided upon their desired field by the 5th or 6th grade. Therefore, the earlier you can expose students to STEM topics in an engaging and exciting way as we do with the CyberPatriot Elementary School Cyber Education Initiative, the greater likelihood they will pursue a STEM path.

UNIVERSITY PARTNERSHIPS

Northrop Grumman is actively engaged with universities across the country to provide an industry perspective on cyber curriculum and degree programs to prepare students for real-world challenges. We helped launch the Nation's first cyber honors program at the University of Maryland—College Park called ACES, the Advanced Cybersecurity Experience for Students. ACES is a living learning community for exceptional students from a variety of majors to enhance their cyber studies. We've also assisted in creating the Nation's first undergraduate Cybersecurity Engineering degree at George Mason University in Fairfax, Virginia. Further, at the University of Maryland—Baltimore County (UMBC), we are providing grants to students from diverse academic and socio-economic backgrounds to pursue cybersecurity education. At great schools ranging from Cal Poly Pomona to the University of Cincinnati and dozens of others across the country our employees are actively engaged in helping to develop curriculum, fund hands-on student projects, and educate future cyber professionals.

DIVERSITY

Because cyber is such a complicated and dynamic challenge, we need a work force that brings with it diversity of thought, culture, education, experience, and problem solving—diversity drives innovation and breeds success. Diversity is truly a strategic asset. Working with university and professional organizations that cater to diverse populations is a great way to attract cyber employees and build a stronger, ethnically and racially diverse work force. We partner with the Society of Hispanic Professional Engineers, Women in Technology, Women in Cyber Security, and Society of Women Engineers to name just a few organizations. We need to ensure that young girls, minorities, and other underrepresented populations recognize that they are welcome and can succeed in the cyber work force. This past year working with a small, disadvantaged business located in Baltimore, Maryland we developed the Cyber Warrior Diversity Program at Morgan State University and Coppin State University, two Historically Black Colleges and Universities (HBCU). This training is designed to prepare individuals to defend information systems and networks by training, testing, and providing certifications in accordance with the DoD Information Assurance Workforce Improvement Program. Additionally, the Northrop Grumman Foundation is funding a 3-year, $2 million program with the National Society of Black Engineer's (NSBE) designed to expand the Nation's engineering work force through a partnership with Historically Black Colleges and Universities (HBCUs). The Northrop Grumman Corporation/NSBE Integrated Pipeline Program will provide 72 engineering students with $8,000 scholarship grants, internships with Northrop Grumman and year-round academic and professional development support. The program's three HBCU partners—Florida A&M University, Howard University, and North Carolina A&T State University—will receive grants, technical assistance, and a package of programs researched and managed by NSBE.

Expanding the diversity of the cyber work force is critical to not only ensuring that we have a sufficient number of cyber professionals but also the range of perspectives and backgrounds necessary to counter a constantly-evolving threat.

BREAKING BARRIERS

I am honored to be here today representing Northrop Grumman and proud of our company's efforts to help develop a robust pipeline of innovative thinkers, engineers, and passionate professionals who will secure our Nation's cyber future. A few final thoughts to leave the committee with:

- *Clearances.*—Beyond just a shortage of cyber professionals, there is also a lack of cleared cyber professionals. We need to figure out ways to improve the clearance process to ensure that both the Federal Government and contractors have the cleared employees to do all the critical National security work that is required.
- *More Cyber-Trained Federal Employees.*—Cyber training across the Federal Government is inconsistent. The Federal Governments as a whole needs to put a greater emphasis on ensuring its employees have the cyber understanding and tools to effectively and securely do their jobs.
- *Increased Partnerships and Coordination.*—There is no single answer to addressing the shortage of cyber workers. Continuing to work across academia, Government, and industry is essential to leveraging investments, best practices, and collectively working together to ensure that our great Nation continues to securely grow and prosper in this increasingly digital age.

I would be happy to answer any questions and Northrop Grumman looks forward to working with the committee on this effort.

Thank you again.

Mr. RATCLIFFE. Thank you, Dr. Papay.

The Chair now recognizes Ms. Okafor for 5 minutes.

STATEMENT OF JULIET "JULES" OKAFOR, STRATEGIC ADVISORY BOARD MEMBER, INTERNATIONAL CONSORTIUM OF MINORITY CYBERSECURITY PROFESSIONALS

Ms. OKAFOR. Thank you, Chairman Ratcliffe, Ranking Member Richmond, and Members of the House Homeland Security Subcommittee on Cybersecurity Infrastructure Protection.

I am pleased to appear before you today to discuss the challenges of addressing the severe people problem that hinders our ability to address the advancing threat against our Nation's critical infrastructure.

Technology alone cannot bridge the increasing skills gap our Federal Government continues to face in recruiting and retaining highly skilled cybersecurity talent. Similar to the private sector, it is our belief that the Federal Government must take a more innovative approach to the recruitment and retention of our future cyber work force.

My name is Juliet Okafor, J.D., vice president of business development for Fortress Information Security and Strategic Advisory Board member for the ICMCP, the International Consortium of Minority Cybersecurity Professionals. I am the first black and female employee of Fortress Information Security, a minority-owned cyber risk, intelligence, and management start-up based in Orlando, Florida.

Fortress was founded in 2015 by two entrepreneurs who thought to apply practical business intelligence to address the most complex and emerging challenges across IT, OT, and third-party risk management facing the global critical infrastructure. Our approach for the market, bundling analytics-enabled security-risk orchestration technology, risk governance, and the people. It stemmed from the constant concern reported by CISOs of the world's largest organizations about their ability to hire skilled security staff to fill critical technical security roles.

In May 2016, I joined the International Consortium of Minority Cybersecurity Professionals as the first female co-chairwoman of the Strategic Advisory Board. I lead strategic planning and roadmap development for strategic initiatives, partnerships, and community outreach.

In this role, spend much of my time listening to the efforts taken by the largest global corporations, small businesses, and educational institutions regarding building a talented, diverse, highly diverse, and innovative cyber work force, and then identifying opportunities, programs, tools, and processes that we can implement with these enterprises to leverage and expand diversity-inclusion programs.

The key organizational objectives of ICMCP are, No. 1, to increase the number of female and minority students pursuing cybersecurity-related disciplines at both the undergraduate and postgraduate levels by funding scholarship opportunities; facilitate the career advancement of existing member cybersecurity practitioners through mentoring and grants leading to advanced degrees and/or professional certifications in the field of cybersecurity; promote public awareness of cybersecurity and the opportunities for minorities and underrepresented groups in the profession; No. 4, function as a representative body on issues and developments that affect the careers of minority and women cybersecurity professionals; No. 5, establish a mechanism for gathering and disseminating information toward minorities and underrepresented groups.

In my testimony today, I will highlight the challenges being faced across the public and private sectors in recruitment and retention of cybersecurity talent. These challenges are compounded for diverse populations which face issues with career investment for existing diverse practitioners and retention challenges that also exist in keeping diverse talent once they are recruited.

I will also discuss the efforts and progress made by large and small enterprises, grassroots and nonprofits, like the organizations I represent today, and the efforts that they are making to address the cybersecurity industry's largest and most critical vulnerability, the human factor.

Our research shows that these challenges extend across Government and private sector with scarce talent in high demand, making it even more critical to focus efforts on increasing capacity.

As noted in the Cybersecurity National Action Plan and 2017 budget, the goal remains to identify, recruit, develop, retain, and expand the pipeline of the best, brightest, and most diverse cybersecurity talent for Federal service and for our Nation.

Additionally, a 2014 CIA Diversity in Leadership Study commissioned by the director of the CIA, one of the Nation's largest intelligence and security agencies, said that the lack of diversity in its leadership ranks is of great concern and that diversity is critical to the mission.

The agency further stated that a lack of diversity of thought and experience was identified by Congressional committees and independent commissions as a contributing factor to past intelligence failures and that diversity is mission critical is no longer a debatable proposition, if it ever was.

I thank you for allowing me to speak with you today.

[The prepared statement of Ms. Okafor follows:]

PREPARED STATEMENT OF JULIET "JULES" OKAFOR

SEPTEMBER 7, 2017

Thank you Chairman Ratcliffe, Ranking Member Richmond, and Members of the House Homeland Security Subcommittee on Cybersecurity and Infrastructure Protection. I am pleased to appear before you today to discuss the challenges of addressing the severe "people problem" in addressing the advancing threat to our Nation's critical infrastructure. Technology alone cannot bridge the increasing skills gap our Federal Government continues to face in recruiting and retaining highly-skilled cybersecurity talent. Similar to the private sector, it is our belief that the Federal Government must take a more innovative approach to the recruitment and retention of our future cyber work force.

My name is Juliet Okafor, JD, vice president of business development for Fortress Information Security and strategic advisory board member for the International Consortium of Minority Cybersecurity Professionals (ICMCP). I am the first black and female employee of Fortress Information Security, a minority-owned, cyber risk intelligence and management start-up based in Orlando, Florida. Fortress was founded in 2015 by two serial entrepreneurs, who sought to apply practical business intelligence to address the most complex and emerging challenges across IT, OT, and Third-Party Risk Management, facing the global critical infrastructure. Our approach to the market—bundling analytics-enabled security risk orchestration technology, risk governance, and people stemmed from the constant concern reported by CISO's of the world's largest organizations about their ability to hire skilled security staff to fill critical technical security roles.

In May 2016, I joined the International Consortium of Cybersecurity Professionals as the first female co-chairwoman of the Strategic Advisory Board and chair of the fundraising committee for ICMCP. I lead strategic planning and roadmap development for strategic initiatives, partnerships, and community outreach. In this role, I spend much of my time listening to the efforts experienced by the largest global corporations, small businesses, and educational institutions regarding building a talented, diverse, and innovative cyber work force. Then identifying opportunities, programs, tools, and processes that enterprises can leverage to expand diversity and inclusion programs.

ICMCP's the key organizational objectives are to:

1. Increase the number of female and minority students pursuing cybersecurity-related disciplines at both the undergraduate and post-graduate levels by funding scholarships opportunities.

2. Facilitate the career advancement of existing member cybersecurity practitioners through mentoring and grants leading to advanced degrees and/or professional certifications in the field of cybersecurity.

3. Promote public awareness of cybersecurity and the opportunities for minorities in the profession.

4. Function as a representative body on issues and developments that affect the careers of minority cybersecurity professionals.

5. Establish a mechanism for gathering and disseminating information for minority cybersecurity professionals.

In my testimony today, I will highlight the challenges being faced across the public and private sectors in recruitment and retention of cybersecurity talent. These challenges are compounded for diverse populations, which faces issues with career advancements for existing diverse practitioners and retention challenges that also exist in keeping diverse talent once they are recruited. We will also discuss the efforts and progress made by large and small enterprises, and grassroots non-profits like the organizations I represent today, Fortress Information Security and ICMCP, have made in addressing the cybersecurity industry's largest and critical vulnerability—the human factor.

Our research shows that these challenges extend across Government and private sector, with scarce talent and high demand, making it even more critical to focus efforts on increasing capacity. As noted in the Cybersecurity National Action Plan and 2017 Budget, the goal remains " . . . to identify, recruit, develop, retain, and expand the pipeline of the best, brightest, and most diverse cybersecurity talent for Federal service and for our Nation." Additionally, a 2014 CIA Diversity in Leadership study commissioned by the director of the CIA, one of the Nation highest intelligence and security agency cited that the lack of diversity in its leadership ranks is of great concern as diversity is "critical to the mission". The agency further stated that "a lack of diversity of thought and experience was identified by Congressional committees and independent commissions as a contributing to past intelligence failures . . . that diversity is mission-critical is no longer a debatable proposition—if it ever was".

THE SHORTAGES IN THE CYBERSECURITY WORK FORCE DIVERSITY

According to Frost & Sullivan's 2017 International Information Systems Security Certification Consortium (ISC) Global Information Security Workforce Study (GISWS) of over 19,000 information security professionals globally, across 170 countries, women represent only 11 percent of the total cybersecurity work force despite a projected work force shortfall of 1.5 million people during the next 5 years due to a lack of trained professionals. The percentage representation of African Americans and Hispanics in cybersecurity has been reported at approximately 12 percent combined, for both these groups. This data takes on added meaning when we consider the projected growth in the U.S. minority population over the next few decades where the Hispanic population is expected to grow to 28.8 percent of the U.S. population and the African American population is expected to climb to almost 20 percent according to Census data reflecting population growth 2014–2060.

In a recent USEOC Report, projections for selected STEM occupations with fast employment growth, projected 2012–22, Information Security Analysts have a 37 percent projected growth rate (currently 75,100 jobs annually and 102,500 jobs created annually by 2022), with a Median Annual Wage in 2013 of $88,590.00. Global Information Security Workforce Sub-Reports issued by various industry groups (to include (ISC)2) cite the consistent underrepresentation of African Americans and Hispanics in STEM careers. Only some 6 percent of STEM workers are African American compared to an overall 10 percent of the U.S. work force. Similarly, Hispanics comprise only 7 percent of the STEM work force while making up 15 percent of the U.S. work force. In the past, human bias was understood to be largely a conscious and intentional reason for such gross underrepresentation. New research from the fields of neuroscience and sociology now suggest that human biases are largely unconscious and unintentional.

As the demographics of the U.S. population continue to become more diversified, the importance of increasing the participation of women and minorities in the work force becomes of paramount concern. Ashley Tolbert, a recent Information Security graduate from Carnegie Mellon now working in the Bay Area in Cyber Security Operations, writes of her experiences as a student, intern, and professional in the cybersecurity field that "a lack of diversity and inclusion in the information security field is one of the foremost impediments to attracting and retaining diverse talent, which the industry sorely needs. Since cybersecurity is one of the biggest challenges to our Nation's National and economic security and we're facing a major talent shortfall in the industry, strategies to ensure all capable talent regardless of race, ethnicity, or sexual orientation feel welcome and included is important."

This work force shortfall should be of much consternation given that cyber crime and information theft, to include cyber espionage, remain the most serious economic and National security challenges that our country faces. It has also been reported that this under-participation by large segments of our society represents a loss of opportunity for individuals, a loss of talent in the work force, and a loss of creativity in shaping the future of cybersecurity. Not only is it a basic issue of digital diversity and equality, but it threatens our global economic viability as a Nation.

THE ROOTS OF THE CYBERSECURITY WORKFORCE DIVERSITY GOES BACK TO OUR MIDDLE SCHOOLS AND HIGH SCHOOLS

The work force shortfall and the growing diversity gap in the cybersecurity industry in the United States also reflects the broader challenge that the USA faces in science, technology, engineering, and mathematics, or STEM, programs in our schools. Until we can get more students matriculating with STEM-related degrees, these challenges faced within the cybersecurity industry and overall information technology industry will persist. According to the PEW Research "Fact Tank" Report of International Students in Math and Science, American 15-year-olds were ranked 38th out of the 71 countries included in the report. The results were only slightly more encouraging for our 8-year-olds, who were ranked 11th out of the 38 countries included. As a country, we have to be laser-focused on quality and retention in middle and high school STEM programs, as these formative years determine the future talent pipeline for the cybersecurity work force. Strategies and programs are needed to provide significantly more apprenticeship opportunities as well as opportunities in colleges and universities, to include an infusion of Federal resources to support everything from curriculum and faculty development to tuition support.

Chairman Ratcliffe, our STEM imperative cannot be more urgent for minority students when we consider the projected growth of minority populations according to the census data and the reported labor trends citing the fact that over 90 percent of all jobs by 2030 will require information technology skills.

THE IMPERATIVES FOR GRASSROOTS ORGANIZATIONS AND PRIVATE ENTERPRISES

Nonprofits and educations institutions are tackling the cyber divide by creating academic scholarship opportunities to attract more females and students of color into the career field. For existing minority cybersecurity practitioners, ICMCP is deploying strategic mentoring programs geared toward fostering the career growth of junior and mid-level practitioners into becoming the next generation of executive decision makers. Studies by various groups, have underscored the importance of work-based learning programs, mentorship, apprenticeship, sponsorship, and employee affinity groups as key strategic components of successful diversity and inclusion programs and employee retention initiatives.

Toward fulfilling these five key organizational objectives, last year ICMCP was able to accomplish the following thanks to the generosity of our sponsors,
- Awarded 10 Academic Scholarships @$5K
- Awarded 5 Certification (average $3K)
- Awarded 1 Executive Development ($16K)
- Placed 12 interns in cybersecurity positions
- Matched 17 Protégés to Mutually-Matched Mentors
- Assisted and facilitated the job placements of over one dozen minority cybersecurity professionals at various levels in several industries
- Implemented the first operational Security Operations Center (SOC) at an academic institution toward ensuring students graduate with hands-on skills to augment their classroom learning.

So far in 2017, ICMCP has already accomplished the following:
- Awarded over $100K in academic scholarships,
- Awarded at least 10 certification vouchers (ISC2, CompTIA, SANS, ISACA, IAPP),
- Coordinated the placement of 15 interns and 20 job-seekers.

We should also mention our participation in note-worthy and Government-led initiatives diversity underpinnings also tackling the "Great Minority Cybersecurity Divide" which include:

GENCYBER

The National Security Agency's GenCyber program, co-sponsored by the National Science Foundation, sponsors cybersecurity summer camps for students and teachers at the K–12 level. The goals of the GenCyber program are to help increase in cybersecurity and diversity in the cybersecurity career field; help students understand correct and safe on-line behavior and to improve the teaching methods for delivering cybersecurity content in the K–12 curricula. This year the program sponsored 130 GenCyber camps and reached nearly 5,000 students and 1,000 teachers across the Nation.

THE CONSORTIUM ENABLING CYBERSECURITY OPPORTUNITIES AND RESEARCH (CECOR)

The Consortium Enabling Cybersecurity Opportunities and Research (CECOR) funded by the Department of Energy is a collaborative effort among 13 colleges and universities and 2 National laboratories to develop a K–12 pipeline for the cybersecurity work force.

CYBERCORPS SCHOLARSHIP FOR SERVICE (SFS) PROGRAM

SFS is a program designed to increase and strengthen the cadre of Federal information assurance professionals that protect the Government's critical information infrastructure. This program provides scholarships that may fully fund the typical costs incurred by full-time students while attending a participating institution, including tuition and education and related fees. The scholarships are funded through grants awarded by the National Science Foundation, NSF.

But this is clearly not enough. To make significant progress in developing and employing the cybersecurity capacity our Nation needs, we need to be filling over 200,000 cybersecurity jobs annually according to the Frost and Sullivan ISC2 GISWS Report and to be filling these jobs with diverse candidates.

DIVERSITY WINS

Chairman Ratcliffe, several studies have proven that diverse teams wins and specifically in the private sector, diversity has been shown to positively impact bottom-line revenues. In fact recent reports are showing that every incremental percentage point in African American and Hispanic representation at NASDAQ-listed tech companies is linked with a 3 percentage point increase in revenues. If the racial/ethnic diversity of tech companies' work forces reflected that of the engineering talent pool, the sector at large could generate a 20–22 percent increase in revenue—an additional $300–$370 billion each year. Companies with above-median Hispanic representation (currently standing at roughly 5–6 percent of the technical work force) are linked with annual revenues that are 40 percent higher than companies that fall below the median in Hispanic representation. The links between African American representation and revenues were also positive, yet did not show statistical significance.

There is also a linkage between racial/ethnic diversity and operating margins— every 1 percentage point increase in racial/ethnic diversity at a tech company is linked with 0.3—0.4 percentage point increase in operating margins. Extrapolating to the tech sector achieving levels of racial/ethnic diversity that reflect the talent marketplace would be linked with $6–7 billion in additional operating earnings industry-wide, or roughly a 2–3 percent increase in total industry earnings.

These links between diversity and financial performance are not unique to the tech industry—a range of studies conducted in other industries support them. For instance, research published in the American Sociological Review found that firms with high levels of racial/ethnic diversity have more than 98 percent higher sales revenue, serve over 54 percent more customers, are roughly 33 percent more likely to have above-average market share, and are nearly 30 percent.

Our analysis is supported from the commercial sector, by the well-known consulting firm of McKinsey & Company, who conducted a 2015 study of 366 public companies across a range of industries in the United Kingdom, Canada, the United

States, and Latin America. The resulting analysis of the 366 companies revealed a statistically significant connection between diversity and financial performance. The companies with the highest gender diversity were 15 percent more likely to have financial returns that were above their National industry median, and the companies with the highest racial/ethnic diversity were 35 percent more likely to have financial returns above their National industry median. The correlation does not prove that greater gender and ethnic diversity in corporate leadership automatically translates into more profit—but rather indicates that companies that commit to diverse leadership are more successful.

CONCLUSION

Mr. Chairman, in closing, there are lots of vital efforts underway to tackle the problem we have titled the "The Great Diversity Divide" and progress is being made. Sadly however, with over 250,000 unfilled jobs in cyber each year, with the average representation of women in the cybersecurity industry averaging barely 10 percent for the past few years, same with the combined representation of African Americans and Hispanics with 1 or 2 percentage points, there is much more that can be done and that must be done when we consider the projected minority population growth and trends in the labor market.

Thank you for the opportunity to testify before you today, and I look forward to any questions that you have.

Mr. RATCLIFFE. Thank you, Ms. Okafor.

I now recognize myself for 5 minutes for questions.

I want to start out by thanking you all again for your very thoughtful opening statements.

Dr. Chang, I want to start with you because I know in addition to your prior Federal experience at NSA you are now essentially on the front lines teaching and educating our future cyber work force. Therefore so I would like your perspective on whether working for a larger purpose factors into whether students will choose to serve the Government. In other words, does the potential of protecting our homeland and working at a Classified level, incentivize students and young people?

Mr. CHANG. Yes, I believe it is. I on occasion have the opportunity to chat with students about career choices, about, you know, individual opportunities they may seek. It would be fair to say that for a number of the students they believe that there is potentially something larger than just salary. Now, clearly salary will have a bearing, but I did have one particular student, who, by the way, is a veteran, a former Marine, the guy is a rock star. He is a terrific cyber performer. Any company represented here I think would really enjoy having him. He specifically made the point that for him and many people that he knows would basically choose mission over money.

They want to have an impact, they want to make a difference. They are trained, they are ready, they want to get in the game. To the extent that they understand that, whatever organization will allow them and their skills to make a difference, they would absolutely raise the hand.

Mr. RATCLIFFE. Terrific, thank you.

Mr. Montgomery, with so much focus in recent years about expanding cyber educational opportunities, like we have talked about and in your opening statement as well, why do you think the cyber skills gap is getting worse?

Mr. MONTGOMERY. Well, demand. Think about what is under control of most organizations. They control the number of people that they can hire. They control the budget for technology. Another static factor is the number of hours in the day, that doesn't change.

But think about what does change dynamically. The number of systems that you use in your own household, for example, rages beyond control.

I remarked to a reporter today I have five more IP-enabled devices in my book bag today than I did 5 years ago. I don't see that trend diminishing. So demand, and I don't mean demand for the skills of the personnel, I mean the demand upon those personnel themselves.

So if you have these dynamic factors, the number of systems, the attacks against those systems, the lucrative nature of cyber crime, the interconnectivity of devices to just about everything these days, it creates an untenable math problem that the practitioner can't solve by himself.

So we don't have enough kids coming in, we all know that, but we are also making the existing problem of the existing practitioner worse because of the raw demand of computer power.

Mr. RATCLIFFE. Terrific, thank you.

Dr. Papay, what programs have you found to be most effective for your company's recruiting and retention efforts? Are there metrics at Northrop Grumman that are used to judge the success and failure of recruitment and retention programs?

Obviously, one of the purposes of this is that we are trying to learn from some of the private-sector best practices and whether or not those can apply or should apply in the Federal sector.

Mr. PAPAY. Thank you, Mr. Chairman. So we approach the problem just like any other business would. Where do you want to spend your money? Where do you want to invest your time and energy in looking at, first of all, the recruiting side and then on the retention side. So let me just give you a few numbers, like, some metrics that we look at for Cyber Patriot, for instance.

If we look at the Cyber Patriot participation of the students that are coming in there in the middle schools and high schools, about 87 percent of the kids that are in that program go on to pursue a STEM degree in college. That is a pretty good number.

Then you look at how many of those kids go on and get a college degree and come to work at big companies or go work for the Government, then how long can you keep them with the company? So we look at numbers, like, something like a 92 percent of those kids that come out of the Cyber Patriot Program and then come in to work for Northrop Grumman as an intern or as a summer hire, about 92 percent of them come back again and stay and either continue their education or continue their career with us or both.

So you have got to think about where you want to invest your money and where you want to spend the time. I think the Federal Government can look at that like a business.

Mr. RATCLIFFE. Terrific.

My time is expired.

The Chair now recognizes the Ranking Minority Member for his questions.

Mr. RICHMOND. Sure.

Dr. Chang, I will just start with a comment where you are. So if you look at SMU, whose tuition is, give or take, somewhere around $45,000 a year, not including room and board, the demand upon students as they come out of college now, the financial demand is a serious obstacle as we talk about—maybe somebody has a solution for it. Who knows?

So the question becomes, and I think that you are right when you start talking about supply and demand and you start talking about the overall good of the country, demand is so high right now, whether you are talking about Samsung and a refrigerator that hooks up to the internet of things or you are talking about my sous vide device where I can cook over wifi in my home while I am here in the District of Columbia and it is in New Orleans.

So the demand is very extraordinary, which then the supply is still limited and it is going to be limited for a while. So the question I have is, as Government, how do we think outside the box? How do we do things in a creative manner to create some capacity? How do we compete for those students who have a number of challenges that they have to deal with?

Just as a side, do you know any State or local governments that are doing a good job at retention or recruitment?

Mr. CHANG. I will offer a couple of thoughts. So I think there is sort-of this notion of top-down and bottom-up. So the bottom-up perspective basically says when students graduate they kind-of know and follow where the other students go. So if they join a company or an organization and the students say, hey, that is a really great place, come join me, they sort-of keep track of each other. So there is this sort-of bottom-up perspective that if you get some number of students, they may attract some others.

I think there is also sort-of a top-down perspective as well that says if DHS, for example, were able to recruit a really big-name cyber professional, that would be a little bit of a magnet for some other students. So I think maybe some Fortune 500 CISO or something like that or some big name out of Government, I do think the students would say, gosh, that is somebody I admire, that is somebody I respect, somebody I can learn from, might be an interesting strategy as well.

Mr. RICHMOND. Anyone else?

Ms. Okafor.

Ms. OKAFOR. Thank you. I believe that cybersecurity has a branding problem. One of the biggest inhibitors in my conversations with students and practitioners looking to enter the field from non-IT-related industries is that it is mostly military or it is seen as highly technical with penetration testing. It sort-of in some situations lacks the kind of cool that I think a lot of millennials are looking toward when they are looking to build out their career.

Then when you talk about the Federal Government and you think about some of the issues that we are facing in society today, some people are reticent to enter something that both seems very, you know, sort-of situated around military and then institutionally-based.

So one of the things that I noticed is, a number of years ago when I, and I won't share my age, but when I was growing up, I saw a number of commercials as a young black woman who grew up in Brooklyn about the military and the benefits the military had very early on. For a commitment up front, you got a lot on the back end. I think cybersecurity needs to really start to broaden its awareness of the opportunities in it and get people to invest in the mission very early on.

That will then allow them to, as they are being sort-of approached by other industries, it is not just the money because they are aware of what the benefits are and they also understand what the task is that they would be a part of. So I think that would be much more helpful with regards to the branding issue I see.

Mr. RICHMOND. Thank you. I guess just from my perspective, and you all can just tell me if you agree, part of it is just that when you work for Government it is so rigid. When you are in the cybersecurity space or really coding space or whatever you want to call it, you know, the days of wearing a suit, the days of all of this structure are really going away because people have the ability to work anywhere and work in any kind of environment.

Are we perpetuating our own barrier by our traditional means of how we think about the workplace as opposed to what technology offers?

With that, Mr. Chairman, I will yield back.

But, you know, a yes or a no or a sentence would help.

Mr. PAPAY. Yes. I will expand a little bit. One of the things that I think, and to Ms. Okafor's point, cyber doesn't know boundaries, it doesn't know buildings, it doesn't know facilities, it doesn't know data centers, it doesn't know anything. It knows where the demand is. So the notion of going to this same cube to work on something that affects someone in Ohio versus Montana versus Texas, it is a little bit at cross purposes, absolutely.

Mr. RATCLIFFE. All right.

The Chair now recognizes the gentleman from Rhode Island, Mr. Langevin.

Mr. LANGEVIN. Thank you, Mr. Chairman. I want to thank you for holding this hearing.

I want to thank our distinguished panel for being here. I appreciate the contributions that each of you have made in your own right to advancing the field of cybersecurity.

So, Mr. Chairman, in March, NICE, National Initiative for Cybersecurity Education, issued a request for information on scope and sufficiency of efforts to educate and train the Nation's cybersecurity work force. I responded to highlight several areas that I hope that they will focus on.

I ask unanimous consent, Mr. Chairman, if I could, that the letter that I sent to be included in the record as context for my questions for this distinguished panel.

Mr. RATCLIFFE. Without objection.

[The information follows:]

LETTER FROM HON. JAMES R. LANGEVIN

AUGUST 1, 2017.

Ms. Danielle Santos,
Cybersecurity Workforce RFI, National Institute of Standards and Technology, 100 Bureau Drive, Stop 2000, Gaithersburg, MD 20899.

DEAR MS. SANTOS: The National Institute of Standards and Technology has requested information on the scope and sufficiency of efforts to educate and train the American cybersecurity work force of the future. Investment in our nation's cybersecurity work force is crucial to our national and economic security, and I write to applaud NIST for its efforts in this matter. While we often focus on the technologies that result from research, it is at least as much the skilled work force behind the breakthroughs that drives our country forward.

Unfortunately, we are far behind where we need to be. Within the cybersecurity work force today, we have hundreds of thousands of jobs unfilled, thereby limiting our ability as a nation to respond to the malicious actors who daily target our infrastructure, finances, and intellectual property. We need short-, medium-, and long-term solutions that reach all components of the educational pipeline from K–12 education to university programs to certifications. We also need to explore retraining and apprenticeships as ways to infuse additional talent into the field.

In order to properly understand the scope of the challenge, it is crucial that NIST applies measures and metrics to the cybersecurity work force, and I was pleased to see their inclusion within the request. As a nation, we must analyze the expected demand for cybersecurity personnel, the efficacy of training programs in producing skilled workers, and the ability of our educators, both in number and in capability, to instruct students. Furthermore, we must share across our communities the lessons and best practices learned from these studies to ensure that students throughout the nation have access to the best cybersecurity education possible no matter where they live.

Additionally, the dynamic nature of technology development ensures that even our best-laid plans will require adaptation as innovative technologies come on the market. This is perhaps one of the most significant challenges that we will face in shaping tomorrow's work force, and it will require novel approaches to training. The emerging use of artificial intelligence to assist cybersecurity tasks, for example, may dramatically alter the tasks of a computer and network security engineer in the coming decades. Similarly, the rapid growth in connected devices may create new classes of cybersecurity professionals focused on the unique challenges posed by the Internet of Things. We must prepare our work force for this future while also preparing them to be adaptable to the disruptions that we expect but cannot predict.

Only by continuing to invest in our skilled work force will we be able to ensure our nation's continued security and prosperity in the digital economy. This request for information is a positive contribution to understanding where the work force is today and what we must do in the future. I thank you for your leadership on this issue and I look forward to the results of your request.

Sincerely,

JAMES R. LANGEVIN,
Member of Congress.

Mr. LANGEVIN. Thank you, Mr. Chairman.

So to the panel, in all of your testimony, you point out that there is a strong demand signal for more cybersecurity workers. Yet, and you in particular, Dr. Chang, can appreciate as one of the members of the CSIS task force with me and Chairman McCaul, and I thank you for your work there, but understand that this is not a new problem. The demand signal really has existed for well over a decade now. One of the biggest challenges that policy makers have faced, in my view, is figuring out why there really hasn't been more of a market-driven response to the shortage.

So based on your experiences, why has the cybersecurity work force gap lagged behind the broader computer science gap which has seemed much more responsive to the growing demand for software engineers?

Mr. CHANG. Yes, so a couple of things. So I think it is very thoughtful when you make a comparison between cybersecurity and computer science. The field of computer science as a major has been around for many years now, as you know. In terms of a specific discipline for cybersecurity, it is very new.

It seems to us that we have been sort-of thinking about cybersecurity for a very long time, but as a discipline distinct from computer science, computer engineering, information technology, it really is very new. So as students begin taking some of these programs from these different universities, they are not getting the same thing.

I mention in my testimony the idea that when universities begin building up their cybersecurity programs there really needs to be a common curricular guidance so that everybody basically says cybersecurity is kind-of the same thing. Because right now it is a little bit of a mix-and-match and so you will, you know, you will get a major or a minor or a certificate or something, but you are not getting quite the same thing.

So it is, you know, still a little bit of a new thing. I think it is now public awareness has raised, but it is still basically a pretty infant discipline.

Mr. LANGEVIN. Thank you.

Mr. MONTGOMERY. I would agree, and I don't want to sound like a broken record, but it is demand. It is demand. The demand for practitioners has far outpaced the ability for the educational system to deliver because we have changed everything. You didn't buy anything on your telephone 10 years ago. Many of us didn't buy anything on the internet 10 years ago. Many of us didn't have broadbands to our house 10 years ago. Certainly, no one had an internet-connected refrigerator or television 10 years ago.

So it is absolutely that I don't think that it is a lack of interest or a lack of programs. I don't think it is a lack of educational institutions offering education. I think it is nascent from the cybersecurity as a discipline standpoint, but we simply have far more demand than our ability to fulfill and that will worsen as more devices are IP-enabled. The Patriot Missile has an IP address while it is in flight. That is going to get worse before it gets better.

Mr. PAPAY. Congressman Langevin, if I may agree with Scott here for a second, I know it doesn't happen often, the demand is building up because all of the things that are out there that are legacy systems as well are now possible attack targets. So you even think about DHS's mission, not just one from a responsibility to provide information out to businesses and Government organizations through US–CERT, but also the work that DHS does in TSA and CBP, all those are opportunities for people who are cyber-trained to become part of DHS's mission and protect the systems that DHS delivers for our Nation. So the demand may be even more than we see up front because of that number of legacy systems that are out there that need protection.

Mr. LANGEVIN. Thank you.

Ms. OKAFOR. I would add a caveat that it is not the demand itself, but the lack of response to the demand, meaning we are not changing fast enough with regard to the systems that we have in place.

For instance, the Ranking Member talked about, you know, sort of the rigidity of the Federal Government. I am often concerned with the kind of education that exists to prepare people for a cybersecurity job. You need more hands-on learning. But often, you are still seeing these certificate programs come up that teach using just books.

So what happens? They graduate school and then it becomes a company's responsibility to invest in training the work force to actually start on Day 1. So there is a gap there because organizations are not quickly responding, due to bureaucracy or politics, to the demand of the new work force.

Then finally, we talk about technology as an enabler, but I want to talk about the fact that technology is engineered by people. Unless we address the fact that people still continue to have unconscious bias and are reticent to change and, therefore, it is impacting our ability to hire quickly enough to bring on the right people to address the demand. Thank you.

Mr. LANGEVIN. Thank you.

I know my time is expired.

I thank all of you for your insights into this. I just, you know, I just see the, you know, the fact that, you know, computer scientists are learning new language, new things are being coded. I mean, the web programming languages are new and apps have only existed for a decade, but, you know, there are plenty of app coders, but we don't see enough market demand moving into cybersecurity, I would say, filling those roles.

So we have a couple hundred thousand openings right now in the cybersecurity field and we just don't—it doesn't seem like that is migrating enough in terms of training enough people in that field, so it is a challenge.

But I know my time is expired. I yield back. I will perhaps have some questions for the panel that I will submit for the record. Thank you.

Mr. RATCLIFFE. Advise the gentleman I intend to have a second round if you are interested in staying around.

The Chair recognizes the gentlelady from Florida, Mrs. Demings.

Mrs. DEMINGS. Thank you so much, Mr. Chairman.

Thank you to our witnesses and welcome.

Particularly to you, Ms. Okafor, who comes from my home town.

What a very interesting topic. I want to thank our Chairman and Ranking Member for it.

Mr. Montgomery, I would just like to go back to what you were saying about demand. You know, I spent a lot of years in law enforcement and we used to talk a lot about being proactive and not reactive. DHS was created 17 years ago or so to change the way we do business. So did we just not see the demand coming? Or did the internet exceed our wildest dreams?

Mr. MONTGOMERY. Can it be both? If I had told you when homeland was founded what you would be able to do from the confines of your pocket and your phone, would you have believed it?

I believe that the pace of technology has accelerated so dramatically in the last 20 years so much faster than the prior 200, the things that we do and take for granted today, they simply didn't exist 10 years ago, 15 years ago, 20 years ago.

So I think it is we are always going to err on the side of availability and progress. There is definitely contention between availability and progress and security and privacy. The practitioner's first job is to say no, you can't do that, it is new, I don't understand it yet. But what do we say as consumers? Hey, I just need it to work. So there is definitely contention.

I don't think the Government missed the boat or missed the size of the problem any more than anyone else did. It is simply a question of the pace outpacing our ability to respond. I don't think that is a Government issue, I think that happens in every organization, whether they are in the private sector or not.

Mrs. DEMINGS. You also talked about a shared work force, if you will, combining a private and public sector employee to do both jobs. I think the pros of that are very, very obvious. Could you talk about some of the cons of having that kind of work environment?

Mr. MONTGOMERY. Well, certainly clearances and the clearance process make it trickier for certain systems to be protected. But let's face it, the overwhelming percentage of systems and the overwhelming percentage of data are Unclassified. Certainly, as the Department moves toward the cloud and embraces that economy of scale like everyone else, that rotating work force could be relegated to the cloud management aspects which are more public. So I think there are ways to offset sort-of the recurring nature or the temporary nature of workers by simply relegating them to more Unclassified roles.

I see tremendous benefit in that a private citizen may not understand what the word "mission" means until they are exposed to it. I am a software engineer by background, but my own exposure to the word "mission" came with involvement in the Department of Defense. I take that word more seriously now than I did when I was a kid in the cube. I think the same thing could be said of these cyber partnerships between the private and public sector.

Mrs. DEMINGS. Thank you.

Ms. Okafor, in a study that was done this year involving women who had worked or working in cybersecurity, over half of them reported that they had been discriminated against in some way. You certainly talked about being a first on more than one occasion. I would like to hear about your own experiences of discrimination within the field and hear some more about what recommendations you would make for employees in the private and the public sector to create an environment that is more conducive to recruiting women and other minorities.

Ms. OKAFOR. I would be happy to share. So it is, you know, it is not easy to be the first black woman, but I wear it as a badge of honor. The biggest areas of discrimination I face tends to be overt. There is a subtlety mostly of a suggestion that I perhaps don't know what I am talking about or perhaps need to be explained.

I find often that I need my male coworkers to vouch for some of my big ideas, unlike some of my male counterparts. So I can't say that in my experience I have faced anything that would sort-of, you know, touch anything near some more overt forms of racial discrimination, but there are lots of conversations that I am not included in because lots of the dealing happens after hours in places that perhaps they don't think I would perhaps be welcome.

So what I suggest for organizations is really starting to question itself. I talk a lot about organizations conducting both third-party and self-assessments of the culture. The culture of an organization is critical, not only with regard to who they are hiring and who is in the organization, but also an unhappy, unproductive work force cannot be a secure work force.

So those two are linked; and therefore, an organization needs to understand how it treats its employees, how it is perceived by the market with regard to attracting employees and then ensuring that they give opportunities for women to be seen as having the right frame of mind, the right thoughts on big projects, to have executives that they can see as being perhaps an ideal that they could perhaps reach.

So I feel like you can no longer separate the need for diversity of thought, gender, racial diversity without also saying that without doing that you are impacting directly the ability to secure the organization, secure the Nation. Thanks.

Mrs. DEMINGS. Thank you so much. I am out of——

Mr. MONTGOMERY. I am sorry, if I can just add briefly.

Mrs. DEMINGS. OK, please go ahead.

Mr. MONTGOMERY. I can't agree enough. No insider threat starts their career as a threat to their organization. It is through cultural pressure, cultural unhappiness. We have seen this at TSA on the front lines. No one starts unhappy. It is their environmental pressures that create insider threat, so I totally agree on checking your culture and reassessing from time to time.

Mrs. DEMINGS. Thank you so much.

Thank you, Mr. Chairman.

Mr. RATCLIFFE. The Chair now recognizes the gentleman from New York, Mr. Katko.

Mr. KATKO. Thank you all for being here. I constantly hear from my constituents back home about this issue, about the whole cybersecurity issue. They are terrified. Getting it right is critically important.

I have really got to commend both of you for the last colloquy you had because it is really important to have the discussions. You can't make change until you identify the problem. Once you identify the problem, then you can address it. So I encourage you to continue to speak up and let us know how we can help, if in any way. So it is a very important issue and keep it up.

But, Dr. Montgomery, I want to talk a bit about the public/private-sector cross-pollinization I call it, pollination, whatever we want to call it. I am very interested in that. I think it is something that can be a very dynamic thing. I am also interested in how we can better expand that and better utilize that moving forward as a way to get people from both the Government sector and the private sector get on the same page more instead of having this more stratified relationship that we have now.

So would you like to comment on that a little bit? I would like to have others as well.

Mr. MONTGOMERY. Sure. So first and foremost, having some industry influence inside the confines of Government is never going to be a bad thing. Exposing permanent Government employees——

Mr. KATKO. So what you are saying is people in Government don't always know everything that is right for industry?

Mr. MONTGOMERY. I would never say it that way specifically.

Mr. KATKO. That is shocking.

[Laughter.]

Mr. KATKO. Well, I am, I am telling you that is why we want to do it.

Mr. MONTGOMERY. But I think that sharing of ideas, there is certainly process in the Government that has to be observed with respect to data classification. But beyond that sort of rigid wall, the whole reason that enterprise works and industry works is because it is allowed to try to solve problems more creatively.

The other thing I think that helps a lot with respect to a visiting work force, so to speak, is the diversity of that work force itself. Many of them will be returning veterans whose experience in the most difficult places on earth lends itself pretty well to crisis situations in a civilian organization as well.

But if you think about visiting professionals, you may wind up having all sorts of diversity, whether it is racial diversity, whether it is more women in the workplace, but that constant influx of new ideas is how problems get solved.

Cybersecurity is almost, when you look at the highest ends of the practitioners, it is almost more like an art than a science and it takes a lot of different points of view. Right now, we don't have enough points of view, including more people who aren't necessarily, "cyber practitioners" to be some of these rotating personnel who will sharpen the ideas of the cyber practitioners, being exposed to those ideas in the cyber workplace.

I can't say enough about how this will help spur new thinking, both in the private sector as well as the public sector.

Mr. KATKO. The Department of Homeland Security has just secured its first loaned executive, as they call it. I think we need more. I say that because even in my subcommittee which I chair, the Transportation and Protective Service Subcommittee, we now have a Secret Service agent that is detailed to us. He is giving us a totally different perspective on the Secret Service side of things.

So I totally agree with it. Now you see a lot of colonels come through here and they do their time, if you will, on Capitol Hill before they become a general. They have to understand how this place works if they are ever going to be able to be effective at their jobs as a general for the most part.

So I would like to hear from you all, not just that it is a good idea. How can we expand it? What can we do better with that? What would you suggest we do?

Go ahead, Dr. Papay, you want to try?

Mr. PAPAY. Sure. So one of the things that as you are facing this big demand, a shortage of people, we are never going to fill the gap by just continuing to funnel new kids in the bottom. You are not going to get to 1.8 million jobs in 2022 doing it that way. So the importance of information sharing now becomes clear in our role as cyber defenders. I share information on a tactical level and a strategic level with both my defense industrial base partners and the Government counterparts.

We need to adopt a much more broad information-sharing approach that takes advantage of the fact that my folks now don't have to find every threat targeted at my company because somebody else over there found that threat first, let me know about it, and I put it in automatically, automatic information sharing, I am up, I am good, and I am protected. So I think scalable solutions are the key and information sharing is one of those.

I don't think we realized it at the time when we were thinking about, hey, we have got to get information sharing more broad. It is a scalable solution that helps us solve that gap.

Mr. KATKO. Ms. Okafor.

Ms. OKAFOR. I would agree with him. Two of the examples that I have seen that work really, really brilliantly is when you have the public and private sector actually collaborate around a goal. I have seen cyber exercises in particular industries, so, for instance, maritime security via U.S. Coast Guard. They have been doing these exercises all across the country where they are inviting U.S. Coast Guard cybersecurity professionals in addition to industry and they are actually doing exercises together. So they can each come to the table with what they know and actually solve a problem.

I have also seen this done with GridEx, which is an initiative led by the Department of Energy, and all of the energy companies who are naturally sharing information, they come together to work to do tabletop exercises, cybersecurity workshops, and this is an opportunity in a much more informal setting to actually have a real conversation.

I think the problem with the public and private sector, they speak different languages. Oftentimes in these very rigid, hierarchical structures, people are not willing to share. So these are some of the things I have seen in real life that actually have people leave and they feel much more enlightened than they started.

Mr. KATKO. Thank you.

Dr. Chang, anything?

Mr. CHANG. Yes. I will mention information sharing, though, in a different way. So at our university, there is a security group where students meet on their own time voluntarily once a week to basically share information with each other. You see that they are exploring different career options.

One of the sessions they have is to basically bring companies in to kind-of describe what those companies do. So when you are a student, maybe you have heard of Google or Facebook or Microsoft or something, you probably haven't heard of DHS or TSA or, you know, Customs and Border Protection or something.

So the extent to which students find out that, gosh, working at this particular organization has a really cool cyber mission, they just wouldn't know. So the extent that you can kind-of get the word out there I think would be quite appealing.

Students really do, they are sponges, they are soaking it up. So they actively seek information. If the word got out there a little bit more that there is an interesting cyber mission, that would be helpful.

Mr. KATKO. It just seems to me that a great way to do it is with cross-pollinization. I hope we can continue to expand this. If there are ideas you think about later of what we can do to incentivize that or do something, it should go both ways.

I mean, we would want people from Capitol Hill to come work in industry for 6 months and see that side of it as well. It would definitely give them a different perspective, especially as the pay disparity between the two, so maybe that is not such a good idea.

[Laughter.]

Mr. KATKO. But it is very, very important. I encourage you all to partake in it as best you can. We are going to endeavor to do the same.

With that I yield back, Mr. Chairman.

Mr. RATCLIFFE. Thank you.

The Chair now recognizes the gentlelady from California, Ms. Barragán.

Ms. BARRAGÁN. Thank you, Mr. Chair.

I represent a majority minority district. It is about 75 percent Latino and African American. I recently read a report that said only about 12 percent of the information security work force was made up of African Americans, Asian Americans, and Latinos. What is the cybersecurity industry doing to ensure a more representative work force?

Go ahead, you want to start?

Ms. OKAFOR. OK. So yes, the fact you stated is completely correct. The activities are disparate, and I think that is part of the problem is not a lot of the organizations are working together. But what we are seeing from the large organizations, like a McAfee, like Google, Facebook, what they are doing is most recently Google actually put a new Howard University campus on its campus in order to start to raise awareness of minority students about the opportunities at Google.

What we have also seen is a rise in those organizations sponsoring HBCU programs, doing college tours that take into consideration HBCUs and primarily Hispanic-serving institutions.

What they are attempting to do is, instead of expecting, as in the past, that minorities and women find them, they are actually going out into those communities and using the channels that they know those communities actually look to for additional information.

What they are also trying to do is sort-of broaden overall awareness with, you know, sort-of social activism, things that, you know, that represent strongly with women, taking part in some of the urban community events that they might not typically be seen.

Then more than anything, actually doing career days where they are having their employees go on-site, do either lunch-and-learns that I have seen or they are actually doing workshops with some of the students just to talk to them about the opportunities.

So the activities have not been combined and I think that might be part of the problem. But what I have seen is a frequency, an increasing amount of frequency in the activities that they are conducting.

Ms. BARRAGÁN. So the district I represent also is a very low-income community. Median income is about $44,000. Only about 11 percent of students go on to college. So everything I am hearing is having the word "college" in it, you know, on colleges it is happening. You are telling me, you know, a lot of college tours. What about the students who don't want to do a 4-year? What kind of opportunities are there for them in this work force? What can we do to make sure that they are not left out?

Before I let you answer, you know, I used to be on a council in a very affluent city called Hermosa Beach. They had something called UCode, and you could sign up as a student and you could go after school. It was not—it was expensive. Even people there said it was not affordable. You don't see anything like that in Compton or Watts where I represent. Certainly, it would be very challenging for people there to send their kids to something that is so expensive. So what can we do to make sure we don't leave these communities out?

Mr. PAPAY. So, ma'am, another great example of that is a partnership we just started with the National Society of Black Engineers where, like you say, you reach out to them through these societies where you can reach a larger population. This is a—it is an integrated pipeline program to provide 72 engineering students with $8,000 scholarship grants at historically black colleges and universities.

You don't have to go to a 4-year university to get into the cyber program. You know, we are hiring kids in high school and getting them started that early. Then if they want to stop after 2 years and then work on some certifications, that is what you need to get started in cyber.

Then you continue and if they are interested and they want to go on for a further degree, great, we will support that. But you have got to reach in to them early and say here is an opportunity for a scholarship. If you don't have a lot of money, a great chance to go to a school nearby and get started.

Ms. OKAFOR. Also, the idea of the lack of, you know, either the pipeline or the lack of ability to track talent often comes down to dollars and cents. The digital divide is a big issue with the number of minorities and Latino students not having the same access to technology at a younger age as some of their white counterparts or white peers.

So a number of institutions, like Symantec, they are donating some of their technology to schools in areas with primarily under-represented groups. I have seen that quite a bit.

The other thing that I am seeing is a rise in the number of apprenticeships that are available to either students of vocational programs and junior colleges or high school students who demonstrate an ability to pass a certain criteria or a test.

In doing so, what they are doing is building loyalty to the organization early on, but they are also creating hands-on learning that will allow them to be ready on Day 1 with the organization making the initial investment in that talent and saying we think you are important enough to invest our money and our resources to train you.

So there is a preponderance of apprenticeships, hands-on learning programs, internships that are focusing on junior colleges, community colleges, and also vocational institutions.

Ms. BARRAGÁN. Great, thank you.

I yield back.

Mr. RATCLIFFE. Thank the gentlelady for coming to our subcommittee hearing.

I am going to exercise my discretion as the Chairman to ask a second round of questions, and I invite any Members that want to do that and I will recognize you as well, really for the purpose of asking one question.

I think we have had a great discourse on some of the areas where we need to focus, some of the solutions. But with respect to the overall goal here, assisting the Department of Homeland Security in accomplishing its cyber mission, I want to make sure that I have given each of you the opportunity to highlight the most important and the most immediate steps that you think DHS can take to mitigate the shortage of cybersecurity workers at the Department.

I know, Mr. Montgomery, that you have identified the CyberCorps, expanding that as one of the things.

It is not intended to be redundant, but I want to make sure that we have captured everything valuable that you all might be able to relate to us.

So I will just go down in order and start with you, Dr. Chang.

Mr. CHANG. OK. So as I mentioned, occasionally I have conversations with students about career choices and so forth. I expressly put to them the question, if you were motivated to work for the Government, what do you think?

So the organizations that kind of rose to the top for them were NSA and FBI. One student actually mentioned that they had watched "CSI: Cyber" on TV and thought that was really cool, so I don't know how many other students watch "CSI: Cyber" but, you know, maybe that sort-of rose, you know, created a little bit more demand for FBI. So I think it is really important, again, to kind-of raise awareness.

Another thing that comes up, and I think this is important, the students come out of school at the top of their game and they are technically really sharp, they kind-of, you know, want to stay sharp. If they thought that they would move to an organization that weren't using the best tools, that didn't have the best people, they would be less motivated to go there.

So I would really encourage the idea that it is a place that is, you know, sort-of at the leading edge, you get to work with really cool people, it has got a great mission. These are some of the thoughts that students have.

Mr. RATCLIFFE. Terrific. Thank you, Dr. Chang.

Mr. MONTGOMERY. So two things I think that are immediate. No. 1, I would echo Dr. Papay's comments on information sharing. If there is an incident at CBP and it is a system that exists in every other portion of the department, CBP should automatically share that information to the rest of the Department, it shouldn't be a discussion, it shouldn't be a committee, it shouldn't be tabled, it should be automatic.

So if a system is attacked, we know the root cause, we know how to protect against that particular attack. All of that should be made available to the rest of the Department immediately, automatically, without anybody having to touch it. There are ways to do that and they don't actually cost that much, they are actually free, so employ them.

The second thing I would say is, we talk about the math problem, there is a finite number of people, there is a finite amount of budget, 24 hours in the day. So anything that reduces the labor on those practitioners has to be employed. The public cloud is part of this, right?

So let us say a system, to secure a system takes one practitioner 10 hours, just making this up. By contracting with a public cloud provider or a hybrid cloud provider like Northrop, the amount of labor that the practitioner has to spend goes down to only 4 hours because the cloud provider is providing 6 hours of that labor, you have to employ those techniques. You are not going to get more workers, we already talked about that, so you have to reduce the amount of labor.

How do you do it? Automation, information sharing, cloud technologies.

Mr. RATCLIFFE. Thank you.

Dr. Papay.

Mr. PAPAY. I think if I could make one additional recommendation, it would be for the new administration at DHS to go back and look at that 2012 Homeland Security Advisory Council Task Force on Cyber Skills report where we laid out 11 recommendations, and refresh it a little bit, look at it again with a new eye and say, hey, that was 5 years ago, how many of these are still valid, how many of these haven't we done, should we pick up a couple more and really push, because that was a lot of effort by a lot of people across academia and Government and industry to participate in that.

Mr. RATCLIFFE. Terrific.

Ms. Okafor.

Ms. OKAFOR. One of the things I think is a key way for the public sector to benefit from the private-sector ingenuity and innovation is USA Jobs. I myself have taken the steps of trying to apply for jobs in the Federal Government and found a job in the private sector. So I can imagine that there are lots of people who perhaps would be interested in working for the Government who just are daunted by the process.

You know, if anything, Google, Facebook, you know, the McAfees and the Northrop Grummans of the world, they have figured some of that stuff out, we don't have to reinvent the wheel. So why not use some of that work that has already been done? So we don't have to completely innovate, we are just enhancing some of the things we know have already been done.

So I would say I do believe that there is some of this that could be focused on technology, but easily the private sector could help with some of the hiring practices through the system currently existing. Thanks.

Mr. RATCLIFFE. Very good.

Would the gentlelady from Florida like to be recognized? Well, very good then.

I really want to thank the witnesses for your insightful, thoughtful, and frankly, very valuable testimony today.

I also want to thank the Members for their questions.

Members of the committee may have some additional questions for some of you and we would ask you to respond to those in writing.

Pursuant to committee rule VII(D) the hearing record will be held open for a period of 10 days. Without objection, the subcommittee stands adjourned.

[Whereupon, at 4:32 p.m., the subcommittee was adjourned.]

APPENDIX

Question 1a. It seems right now that we are waging war against criminals who would hack our systems, and the role of the cybersecurity professional is one of defender. Do you foresee technical solutions that could perform the work that cyber defenders do now?

Answer. I believe we will see continued innovation and investment in technologies that aim to assist the human cyber defender. As was discussed in the hearing, the cyber skills gap is large and growing, so to the extent that technological breakthroughs can be achieved to assist existing cyber defenders would potentially be of great value. In my written testimony I briefly referenced the recent DARPA Cyber Grand Challenge. The goal of the Cyber Grand Challenge was to explore the possibility of actually automating the complex tasks of: (A) Identifying a vulnerability in software, (B) creating a fix (or "patch") for that vulnerability and then (C) implementing that patch, in real time. These are complex and time-consuming tasks to perform for a human cyber defender. The result of this Cyber Grand Challenge demonstrated the progress that could be made in automating these tasks. This was an important and significant result. Did the technology perform at the level of the human experts? No—but the results that were achieved are a positive sign about the sorts of advances that might be possible over time.

The technologies of artificial intelligence and machine learning have been around for decades now but in recent years we have seen some important advances in how these machine learning (deep learning) technologies can assist us in everyday tasks (e.g., visual pattern recognition, language processing). We will see increasing efforts to incorporate these sorts of technologies to assist the human cyber defender. At a very general level the idea would be to have computers process large data sets in an attempt to detect suspicious behavior in the data—in a way that a human might not be able to detect. Its clear why techniques like these will be pursued: (A) Limited numbers of human cyber defenders, (B) growing amounts of data to analyze, (C) the criticality of proactively stopping the attacks before they compromise a network or system. The techniques are far from perfect, but important progress is being made. We are also seeing these and other sorts of technologies being positioned on the inside of networks, again with the intent of detecting anomalous behavior and taking action rapidly. At a much more general level, I am bullish on human innovation and ingenuity in discovering creative ways to harness technology in the aid of human cyber defenders.

Question 1b. What research is being performed in cyber defense tools?

Answer. In the response to the previous question I touched on some types of tools that are being developed to assist the human cyber defender. Indeed there is a whole industry of researchers, inventors, developers, startup companies, large established technology companies and Government labs working on R&D in cyber defense and cyber defense tools. As mentioned earlier, I remain bullish on how creative solutions may be brought to bear on the cyber problem; there are lots of bright and motivated people who are working in this space now. With that said, the efforts to create effective cyber defense tools, in my view, will be improved based on the extent to which they are based on a solid scientific foundation, and this foundation—the science of cybersecurity—has been elusive. The field remains too reactive and after-the-fact. Something bad happens and we have to react afterwards. We lack an adequate understanding of how to construct and compose systems that are fundamentally resilient and secure, based on first principles.[1] A very recent report[2] from the National Research Council (NRC) captures the sentiment very well: "Security science has the goal of improving understanding of which aspects of a system (including its environment and users) create vulnerabilities or enable someone or something (inside or outside the system) to exploit them. Ideally, security science provides not just predictions for when attacks are likely to succeed, but also evidence linking cause and effect pointing to solution mechanisms. A science of security would develop over time, for example, a body of scientific laws, testable explanations, predictions about systems, and confirmation or validation of predicted outcomes." The NRC report continues: "A scientific approach to cybersecurity challenges could enrich understanding of the existing landscape of systems, defenses, attacks, and adversaries. Clear and well-substantiated models could help identify potential payoffs and support of mission needs while avoiding likely dead ends and poor places to invest effort. There are strong and well-developed bases in the contributing disciplines. In mathematics and computer science, these include work in logic, computational complexity, and game theory. In the human sciences, they include work in judgment, decision making, interface design, and organizational behavior."

As the community tasked with developing new cyber defense tools works to innovate and create new and better tools, I think it is equally important that the research community work to advance the scientific foundation that will help to make tomorrow's cyber defense tools even more effective. The NSA sponsors a Science of Security (SoS) effort currently that is actively engaging the open academic community in advancing this foundational research. The activity has defined a set of hard problems as a way to focus the effort. The hard problems include: (A) Scalability and Composability, (B) Policy-Governed Secure Collaboration, (C) Security-Metrics-Driven Evaluation, Design, Development, and Deployment, (D) Resilient Architectures, and (E) Understanding and Accounting for Human Behavior. More detail on the NSA's SoS effort can be found on the NSA website[3] as well as the Science of Security website.[4]

Question 2. You mention that many companies are "training in place" to educate individuals to fill cybersecurity knowledge or skills gaps. While this is a worthy exercise, it takes time. What steps can DHS take now to fill the gap, while embarking at the same time on a retraining program?

Answer. In an effort to bring on cyber talent more quickly, companies are engaging with students at the high school level. With the success of various different cybersecurity competitions at the university level (e.g., the National Collegiate Cyber Defense Competition), cyber competitions have now expanded to include students at the high school level (e.g., Cyber Patriot). One company (and I understand that there are others that are pursuing a similar strategy) is pursuing a strategy to bring on some high school students—who have participated in high school cyber competitions—as summer interns. Upon their high-school graduation, some of these students would be offered full-time positions in the company and the company would support their college education, while they are full-time employees. Perhaps DHS has been looking into this, but if not, it might be a way to augment cyber capability.

On a related topic—given that many of these positions will require the employee to be granted a security clearance, I can comment on one company's thinking about this issue. The company recognizes that the time required for their new employee's security clearance processing to be completed can sometimes be lengthy. As a result they have given a lot of thought about how to ensure that the employee is motivated, productive, and contributing during the security clearance processing period. Via a combination of relevant Unclassified projects and self-learning assignments, the company works hard to introduce the new employee to the company's culture, working environment, etc. such that once the security clearance is granted, the employee can hit the ground running to become as productive as possible, as quickly as possible.

One other thought was triggered by a conversation I had recently with a couple of military reservists who are currently employed as cybersecurity employees in the private sector—along with an article I recently came across.[5] The article describes

---

[1] Schneider, F.B. (2012). Blueprint for a science of cybersecurity. The Next Wave, Vol. 19, No. 2, pp. 47–57, National Security Agency, Ft. Meade, MD.

[2] Millett, L.I., Fischhoff, B., and Weinberger, P.J., (Editors), (2017). Foundational Cybersecurity Research: Improving Science, Engineering, and Institutions, National Academies Press, Washington, DC.

[3] *https://www.nsa.gov/what-we-do/research/science-of-security/.*

[4] *https://cps-vo.org/group/SoS/.*

[5] *https://techcrunch.com/2017/04/18/reservists-and-the-national-guard-offer-untapped-resources-for-cybersecurity/.*

that there are large numbers of folks who serve in the Reserves or National Guard who have cyber skills that could increasingly be brought to bear to expand the pool of qualified cyber workers that are available to the Government, particularly in times of crisis.

One final thought relates to the one above and involves volunteerism. During periods of crisis and emergency, many Americans generously offer their time—and specialized skills—to assist. An example comes from the field of amateur radio (also referred to as "ham radio") where there are many examples of people, who hold an amateur radio license, who assist with communications when conventional communication systems are temporarily down due to a storm, hurricane, or other natural disaster. By analogy, perhaps it would be possible to form a civilian voluntary cyber corps to assist DHS during periods of crisis. The State of Michigan has implemented this sort of notion and describes many benefits.[6]

QUESTION FROM CHAIRMAN JOHN RATCLIFFE FOR SCOTT MONTGOMERY

Question. We heard in the hearing that DHS has to overcome a perception hurdle. What can DHS offer its prospective cyber work force to mitigate this perception besides the importance of its mission?

Answer. DHS needs to think and act more strategically when recruiting cybersecurity talent. It all starts back at DHS—DHS needs to upgrade cybersecurity compensation at all levels to attract the best and the brightest and ensure that these professionals, when they earn it, are fast-tracked to more senior levels. DHS needs to ensure that those professionals that want to stay on the technical track, rather than moving up the management ladder, are likewise given real opportunities for career advancement. DHS needs to customize cybersecurity training and continue to invest in its talented cyber work force to ensure that DHS is seen as an agency that values and trains its people. Finally, DHS needs to stream line its decision making as much as possible to ensure that cybersecurity professionals can work in a fast-paced, exciting environment.

QUESTIONS FROM CHAIRMAN JOHN RATCLIFFE FOR MICHAEL PAPAY

Question 1. We heard in the hearing that DHS has to overcome a perception hurdle. What can DHS offer its prospective cyber work force to mitigate this perception besides the importance of its mission?

Answer. The Department of Homeland Security (DHS) plays an absolutely essential role in providing cyber protection for our critical infrastructure, Government systems, and our way of life. We need to do a better job in communicating the criticality of DHS's cyber responsibilities. I think if the public (and DHS employees) better understood the importance of DHS, it could help ensure that the organization was more respected/ appreciated and subsequently instill a stronger sense of service within its work force.

An additional way to help DHS enhance its ability to attract talent is to build an even more positive campaign around Cyber Grants and the National Science Foundation Scholarship for Service program. Students get college tuition paid in exchange for service after graduation. Since students have a choice of which Federal agency to work, DHS can stand-out among the other agencies by advertising among key target audiences the importance of their mission, their work environment, the enormous opportunities, and professional development programs that make it a great place to work. Cyber Grants is frequently offered at universities with high minority population, DHS could effectively build an even stronger, more diverse, and qualified work force (especially if they focus on institutions ((2-year and 4-year)) with those who have achieved the DHS/NSA Certification of Academic Excellence in Information Assurance Education ((CAE))). Additionally, if DHS hires students out of the CAE2Y program (community college) they could develop an energized, qualified, diverse, and committed work force.

Beyond the importance of its mission, in many ways DHS is on the cutting edge of technology. The Science and Technology, Cyber Division is focused on developing innovative solutions for a wide range of challenges. It might be useful to leverage the exciting work of this organization as a tool to energize the Department's cyber work force.

DHS does unjustly suffer from a perception challenge. However, by doing more to communicate the importance of DHS's role in protecting our National security, strengthening the college recruitment and highlighting the exciting technologies

---

[6] *http://www.michigan.gov/som/0,4669,7-192-78403_78404_78419---,00.html.*

that DHS is involved in, I am hopeful that we can help embolden its cyber work force.

Question 2. What do you think is the main reason that CyberPatriot programs have a 23 percent participation rate for females with 12 percent for the average STEM programs?

Answer. CyberPatriot has higher participation of girls than most programs because, quite simply, it is a focus for both Northrop Grumman and the Air Force Association.

CyberPatriot has grown from 9% female participation in 2009 to 23% girls in 2017. The program offers a fun, team environment that makes it easy for girls to get involved. We encourage all girl teams and provide them registration free of charge. Another reason CyberPatriot has higher female participation is because we recognize that children are determining/considering future academic and career choices by about grade 5–7, if we wait 'til high school, it is too late. That's one critical reason CyberPatriot added the middle school division in the competition—girls have not self-selected out of STEM/cyber fields. In order to open minds even earlier, we created the cyber awareness program (Elementary School Cyber Education Initiative (ESCEI)) for grades K–6. We've sent out more than 6,000 free-of-charge ESCEI packages to academic and other young children's programs, so young girls are getting great exposure to the topic—they think it's a perfectly acceptable and normal academic and career choice.

Lastly, many of Northrop Grumman's women employees spend time volunteering in classrooms and coaching CyberPatriot teams. These women are fantastic role models and help inspire future generations of girls to get involved in cyber. Also, we're targeting women's professional associations (Women in Cybersecurity, Women in Technology, Society of Women Engineers, and others) to not only speak at their conferences about the need for girls in Cyber/STEM but also give them another opportunity for their own outreach.

Getting more girls involved in STEM programs is critical to not only helping girls reach their full potential, but diversity in the cyber field also strengthens our long-term economic and National security.

○